Distributing medical resources

European University Studies
Europäische Hochschulschriften
Publications Universitaires Européennes

Series V
Economics and Management

Reihe V   Série V
Volks- und Betriebswirtschaft
Sciences économiques, gestion d'entreprise

Vol./Bd. 3416

PETER LANG
Frankfurt am Main · Berlin · Bern · Bruxelles · New York · Oxford · Wien

Antje Köckeritz

Distributing medical resources

An application of cooperative bargaining theory to an allocation problem in medicine

PETER LANG
Internationaler Verlag der Wissenschaften

Bibliographic Information published by the Deutsche Nationalbibliothek
The Deutsche Nationalbibliothek lists this publication in the Deutsche Nationalbibliografie; detailed bibliographic data is available in the internet at http://dnb.d-nb.de.

Zugl.: Halle-Wittenberg, Univ., Diss., 2011

3
ISSN 0531-7339
ISBN 978-3-631-62398-5

© Peter Lang GmbH
Internationaler Verlag der Wissenschaften
Frankfurt am Main 2012
All rights reserved.

All parts of this publication are protected by copyright. Any utilisation outside the strict limits of the copyright law, without the permission of the publisher, is forbidden and liable to prosecution. This applies in particular to reproductions, translations, microfilming, and storage and processing in electronic retrieval systems.

www.peterlang.de

"Two roads diverged in a wood, and I--
I took the one less traveled by,
And that has made all the difference."

by Robert Frost

Preface

Allocating scarce resources in medicine has become an important topic in the public discussion. In the German statutory health system we face a situation in which there is not enough money to finance all needs. Financial restrictions force us to use resources wisely. This emphasizes the need of general allocation rules and criteria applied to medical allocation situations. The purpose of this work is to implement and interpret properties of axiomatic bargaining theory to special allocation situations in medicine.

The work and results of this dissertation are strongly influenced by the German research group FOR 655 on "Prioritizing in medicine", especially by the subgroup C04 on equality of chances, justice and efficiency in allocating medical resources. This interdisciplinary group of researchers and therefore part of my work as well are financed by the German Research Foundation (Deutsche Forschungsgemeinschaft, abbr.: DFG). The financial support by DFG is gratefully acknowledged.

My work is also funded by the post graduate fund of Saxony Anhalt (Graduiertenförderung des Landes Sachsen-Anhalt). I truly appreciated this financial stipend because it enabled me to combine the doctorate with my family of two young children.

Most of all I thank Prof. Dr. Dr. Marlies Ahlert for developing the idea of the dissertation together with me and for discussing work in progress. Furthermore, I greatly appreciate her support and motivation in achieving my academic as well as personal goals. Also, I thank Prof. Dr. Dr. Bodo Vogt for agreeing to be a second assessor.

The author would like to thank Daniel Friedrich, Dr. Wolfgang Granigg, Prof. Dr. Bettina Klaus, Dr. Ildiko Lajtos, Prof. Dr. Bettina Schöne-Seifert, Dr. Lars Schwettmann, and Jana Zimmermann for helpful comments and review.

I dedicate this work to my family - to my sons, Jannis and Lennart, who taught me the importance of being a mother, to my husband, Dr. Hagen Köckeritz, for being patient and understanding, and to my parents, Margitta and Jürgen Liesenberg, who encouraged me to use the road less traveled.

Frankfurt am Main, June 2012   Dr. Antje Köckeritz

Table of contents

Table of figures 11
Table of abbreviations 13
Table of symbols 15

1 Motivation 19

2 Scarce resources in the German health system – an overview 23

2.1 Introduction to the German statutory system 23
2.2 Examples of medical bargaining situations 28
2.3 Interdisciplinary discussion of scarce medical resources 33
    2.3.1 Interconnectedness 33
    2.3.2 Notations and Methods from health economics 34
    2.3.3 Results from FOR 655 „Prioritizing in medicine" 36
    2.3.4 A specific medical allocation problem 40
2.4 An introduction to cooperative bargaining theory 41
    2.4.1 The notion of bargaining 41
    2.4.2 The Nash concept 44
    2.4.3 The Nash bargaining solution 46
    2.4.4 The Kalai/Smorodinsky bargaining solution for two groups of patients ($n = 2$) 49
    2.4.5 The Kalai/Smorodinsky bargaining solution for more than two groups of patients (n > 2) 51

3 A cooperative bargaining model for two groups of patients 55

3.1 Introduction 55
3.2 Definition of an allocation problem 56
    3.2.1 An example 59
    3.2.2 A cooperative bargaining problem of chances of success ... 62
3.3 Axiomatic characterization and solution concepts 65
3.4 Results and Conclusion 70

4 A cooperative bargaining model with two patients groups, their individual needs and different group size 73

4.1 Introduction 73
4.2 The model 74
4.3 A cooperative bargaining model 81
4.4 Properties and solution concepts from cooperative bargaining theory 83

4.5 Results and conclusion 92

5 Different types of monotonicity in a cooperative bargaining model of
   distributing medical resources 97

5.1 Introduction... 97
5.2 Monotonicity in patients groups 98
5.3 Monotonicity in number of patients groups 101
5.4 Resource monotonicity.. 108
5.5 Monotonicity in claims.. 115
5.6 Results 121

6 Results and outlook 123

6.1 Theoretical results of the medical allocation problem.............................. 123
6.2 Interpreting the results within a medical context 126
6.3 Outlook 130

Scientific references 133
General references... 141

Table of figures

FIGURE 1.1: GERMAN STATUTORY HEALTH SYSTEM – AN OVERVIEW 24
FIGURE 2.1: A BARGAINING SITUATION 47
FIGURE 2.2: PROPERTY OF INVARIANCE OF POSITIVE AFFINE
    TRANSFORMATION 47
FIGURE 2.3: PROPERTY OF WEAK PARETO OPTIMALITY 47
FIGURE 2.4: PROPERTY OF SYMMETRY..47
FIGURE 2.5: PROPERTY OF INDEPENDENCE OF IRRELEVANT ALTERNATIVES 48
FIGURE 2.6: THE NASH SOLUTION $N(S,0)$ 48
FIGURE 2.7: PROPERTY OF RESTRICTED MONOTONICITY 50
FIGURE 2.8: PROPERTY OF INDIVIDUAL MONOTONICITY......................................50
FIGURE 2.9: THE KALAI/SMORODINSKY BARGAINING SOLUTION 51
FIGURE 3.1: FEASIBLE DETERMINISTIC ALLOCATIONS FOR AN ALLOCATION
    PROBLEM WITH $q=10$, $n=2$, $q_1=3$, $q_2=9$ 59
FIGURE 3.2: A SET OF FEASIBLE CHANCE ALLOCATIONS 60
FIGURE 3.3: A SET OF FEASIBLE CHANCES OF SUCCESS 64
FIGURE 3.4: WEAK (=STRONG) PARETO EFFICIENT SET AND SYMMETRIC
    ALTERNATIVES 67
FIGURE 3.5: BARGAINING PROBLEM (L',r') FOR $N=2$. 69
FIGURE 4.1: FEASIBLE DETERMINISTIC ALLOCATIONS FOR EXAMPLE 1 78
FIGURE 4.2: FEASIBLE DETERMINISTIC ALLOCATIONS FOR EXAMPLE 2 79
FIGURE 4.3: FEASIBLE DETERMINISTIC ALLOCATIONS FOR EXAMPLE 3 79
FIGURE 4.4: A SET OF EXPECTED NUMBER PAIRS OF PATIENTS UNDER
    EXAMPLE 1 80
FIGURE 4.5: DIFFERENT TREATMENT SETS 81
FIGURE 4.6: CHANGING THE REPRESENTATION FROM ALLOCATING TO
    PATIENTS (A) VERSUS ALLOCATING BUDGETARY UNITS (B) 84
FIGURE 4.7: INDEPENDENCE OF THE BARGAINING SOLUTION OF
    IRRELEVANT TREATMENT PAIRS..85
FIGURE 4.8: THE NASH SOLUTION YIELDS IDENTICAL SOLUTIONS FOR
    THREE TREATMENT SETS..87

FIGURE 4.9: TWO PROBLEMS WHEN THE NASH CONCEPT YIELDS DIFFERENT SOLUTIONS 88
FIGURE 4.10: PATIENT MONOTONICITY FOR TWO BARGAINING PROBLEMS T AND T' 89
FIGURE 4.11: KALAI/SMORODINSKY SOLUTION AND NASH SOLUTION 91
FIGURE 5.1: KALAI/SMORODINSKY SOLUTION FOR THREE PATIENTS GROUPS 103
FIGURE 5.2: PROJECTED KALAI/SMORODINSKY SOLUTION FOR THREE PATIENTS GROUPS 104
FIGURE 5.3: DIFFERENT MEDICAL BUDGETS 110
FIGURE 5.4: BUDGET MONOTONICITY 111
FIGURE 5.5: SOLUTION PATHS FOR THE KALAI/SMORODINSKY AND THE NASH CONCEPT 113
FIGURE 5.6: INCREASED CLAIM FOR GROUP 1 116
FIGURE 5.7: KALAI/SMORODINSKY AND NASH SOLUTION UNDER MONOTONICITY IN CLAIMS 118
FIGURE 5.8: SOLUTION PATHS FOR NASH AND KALAI/SMORODINSKY SOLUTION 119

Table of abbreviations

abbr.	abbreviated
AN	Anonymity
B.AN	Anonymity in budget allocations
B.CONT	Continuity in budget allocations
B.INV	Invariance of budget transformation
B.INV'	Invariance of budget transformation for n patients
B.IRR	Independence of irrelevant budget allocations
B.MON	Monotonicity in budgets
B.SYM	Symmetry in budget allocations
B.WPO	Weak Pareto optimality in allocating the budget
B.WPO'	Weak Pareto optimality in allocating the budget for n patients
BVA	Bundesversicherungsamt
C.MON	Monotonicity in claims
CONT	Continuity
DFG	Deutsche Forschungsgemeinschaft
EBM	Einheitlicher Bewertungsmaßstab
FOR 655	Forschergruppe 655 in der DFG
G-BA	Gemeinsamer Bundesausschuss
G-DRG	German diagnosis related groups
GKV	Gesetzliche Krankenversicherung
InEK	Institut für das Entgeltsystem im Krankenhaus
INV	Invariance under positive affine transformation
IMON	Individual monotonicity
IQWiG	Institut für Qualität und Wirtschaftlichkeit im Gesundheitswesen
IRR	Independence of irrelevant alternatives
P.MON	Monotonicity in number of patients
PG.MON	Monotonicity in number of patients groups
POMON	Population monotonicity
QALYS	Quality adjusted life years
RMON	Restricted monotonicity
S.INV	Invariance under positive affine transformation of success probabilities

S.WPO	Weak Pareto optimality of chances of success
S.SYM	Symmetry of chances of success
SGB V	Sozialgesetzbuch V
SYM	Symmetry
VKA	Verband kommunaler Arbeitgeber
WPO	Weak Pareto optimality
ZEKO	Zentrale Ethikkommission

Table of symbols

$<$	is less than
$>$	is greater than
$\leq$	is less than or equal to
$\geq$	is greater than or equal to
$\neq$	is not equal to
$=$	is equal to
$\forall$	for all
$\exists$	there exists
$\in$	is an element of
$\notin$	is not an element of
$\subseteq$	is a subset of
$\subset$	is a subset
$\cap$	Is intersected with
$\prod$	product of
$\sum$	sum of
Max	maximum of
Min	minimum of
ch	convex hull of
α_i	parameter for positive affine transformation
β_i	parameter for positive affine transformation
γ	permutation
Λ	set of all groups V and W
λ	number of sequence
M	Kalai/Smorodinsky solution
μ_i	Kalai/Smorodinsky solution for i
D	group of persons/ patients
A_2	set of allocation problems for a
A	allocation problem
$B^{n+}, B^{2+}, \widetilde{B}^{2+} B^{V+}, B^{W+}$	class of bargaining problems
C	vector of chances
c_i	chance for i to receive treatment

C	set of chance vectors
$\overline{c}_i$	chance of not receiving the medical good for i
D	condition of being treated
$\overline{D}$	condition of not being treated
D	status quo
d_i	status quo for i
E	chance of success
F	set of feasible deterministic allocations
F	bargaining solution
f_i	bargaining solution for i
G	set of feasible deterministic allocations of chances of success
H	allocation rule
I	group of patients
I	person, group
J	group of patients
J	person
K	number of persons
$L, \widetilde{L}, L'$	set of chances of success
L^{SYM}	set of all symmetric allocations of chances of success
L^{WPO}	set of all weakly Pareto optimal allocations of chance of success
$l, \widetilde{l}$	vector of chances of success
$l_i, \widetilde{l}_i$	chances of success for i
$M, \hat{M}$	set of all feasible treatment vectors
M	vector of all feasible treatments
m_i	feasible treatments for i
N	Nash solution
N	number of persons/ patients
$\overline{n}$	maximum number of patients that receive treatment
$\overline{n}_i$	maximum number of patients that receive treatment in group i

P, P'	set of probability distributions
p, p'	probability distribution
q_i	medical claim of i
Q	medical budget
$\bar{q}$	maximum budget allocation
$\bar{q}_i$	maximum budget allocation for group i
$R^{n+}, R^{2+}, \widetilde{R}^{2+}, R^{V'}, R^+$	dimensional space
r, r'	vector of success probabilities without treatment
r_i	success probabilities without treatment for i
S, S', S'_V	alternative set
s	vector of success probabilities with treatment
s_i	success probabilities with treatment for i
$T, T', T'', T''', T'''', \bar{T}$	set of all feasible treatment vectors
$t, \bar{t}, \bar{\bar{t}}, \hat{t}, t^*$	vector of all feasible treatments
$t_i, \bar{t}, \bar{\bar{t}}, \hat{t}, t^*$	feasible treatments for i
t^o	status quo with no treatments
u_i	utility for i
$\bar{X}$	ideal point
$\bar{x}_i$	ideal alternative for i
V	group of 2 persons
v_i	transformation parameter for group i
W	group of three persons
X	vector of feasible deterministic alternatives
x_i	feasible deterministic alternative for i
Y	vector of feasible chances of success
z, z'	alternative pair
z_i, z_i^*, z_i'	alternative z for i

1 Motivation

In the German statutory health system (GKV) allocating medical resources and keeping finances for medical goods and services in balance has become a strenuous task. Over the past years the increasing number of examination methods and medications as well as the aging of population intensified the trade-off in allocating financial resources to different medical areas. Tragic choices, when medical therapies suffice to treat only a fraction of patients are indeed very common, for example, in intensive care, dialysis treatment, and organ allocation. In following years, as technological progress and demographic change proceed, the competition over medical resources is expected to become even more intense. Therefore, it is important to find fair distribution mechanisms that may eloquently solve the medical allocation problems about scarce resources. Ways to deal with restricted resources for medical goods are manifold: to cut or to withhold services such as nursing time or waiting time for a doctor's appointment, to increase contribution fees or co-payments, to give incentive to private insurance. So far, the German statutory health system has experienced different changes in selected medical areas. For example, in dental care we have defined minimal services and a system of co-payments and an incentive to private insurance. In a health system with restricted financial resources, several alternatives of keeping the system in balance may be introduced. Yet it is important to understand the consequences of underlying allocation rules their solutions and properties in order to apply in specific medical allocation situations. The question is, which rule shall be applied in a specific situation, does it yield a unique allocation result, what properties has this rule, e.g. are identical situations treated alike, or what type of fairness does it assure … .

This work contributes to the debate of distributing scarce medical resources. We apply distributive concepts from cooperative bargaining to medical allocation situation and discuss properties and solutions. An important aspect is the interpretation of the results to real medical allocation situations in the German statutory health system.

To begin with, we give general and necessary information about the nature and functions of the German statutory health system in chapter 2. We survey how scientific literature in health economics, philosophy, medicine, and law discusses medical allocation problems. In addition, we define the theoretic fundamentals of our model and introduce the Nash concept, properties and solution concepts from cooperative bargaining theory.

In chapter 3 to 5 we analyze allocation mechanisms from cooperative bargaining theory axiomatically and apply properties and solutions to a specific medical allocation situation. We use a medical allocation problem with a scarce medical good that is perfectly divisible, two patients groups and individual group claims. The model reflects an allocation situation in medicine, such as allocating a medical budget to different departments (patients groups) in a hospital. Each patient group has a medical claim which refers to standard medical treatment in the German statutory health system. The allocation situation is such that each group's claim could be provided but the medical budget does not suffice to satisfy all claims.

Technically, in chapter 3 we define assumptions and notations of the model such as a chance of receiving a medical good and success probabilities under the condition of treatment or no treatment. We introduce a cooperative bargaining problem and apply its notations to a specific medical allocation problem such that we define a bargaining set and a status quo, a bargaining problem, and a solution and its properties in a medical allocation problem. Compared to cooperative bargaining the class of bargaining problems considered in this work is restricted due to thresholds. We present properties and solutions of cooperative bargaining concepts on a subclass of allocation problems. We apply desirable properties, such as Pareto efficiency, symmetry and different types of monotonicity and two allocation mechanisms from cooperative bargaining – the famous Nash and Kalai/Smorodinsky solution concepts.

The following fourth chapter refers to the model in the previous chapter, yet we define a cooperative bargaining problem for two groups and *different group size*. Again, we apply two solution concepts from cooperative bargaining theory and discuss their properties and health-economic implications. We analyze how the variation in the model impacts solution concepts and interpretation of the model.

The fifth chapter discusses different monotonicity properties from cooperative bargaining. The question is how solution concepts react to small changes in the initial conditions. We present a variety of different versions, one of which is budget monotonicity. The question here is how the allocation rule accounts for increasing or decreasing budgets. We motivate their use in a medical context, give definitions and application examples. Especially, we want to find out if their application in a medical context contributes to basic principles and intuitions in allocating medical resources. Further we present sets of properties that characterize either of the two solution concepts.

Besides the technical work of transferring solution concepts and their properties from cooperative bargaining theory to a medical allocation problem, we aim to interpret these properties and solutions in a medical context. An important precondition of the allocation problem is that not all patients may receive standard treatment under a scarce budget. How does this coincide with the general conception that *all* patients ought to be treated? Another important demand is Pareto optimality of the allocation rule. This aspect goes with a general conception of bargaining that after the allocation process no more patients can be treated with the remaining resources otherwise the allocation is considered inefficient. Different interpretations of the allocation result are possible - either to give reduced treatment to all or to refuse treatment to some patients. As we proceed we find answers and examples to it. Important aspects are criteria such as justice, solidarity, and financial ability of the German statutory health system. We also discuss several cuts in services such as length of stay in hospital, time to care per patients, co-payments, private insurance. Last, but not least we discuss a treatment catalogue that constitutes basic services.

In a final chapter we summarize main results of this work in detail and give implication for the German statutory health system and state further research questions.

Within the presented versions of the model we restrict the scope of application to medical allocation situation.

Most importantly we pay attention to distributive solution concepts, their solutions and properties. So we focus on the allocation decision of a medical budget to different health interests. We neither discuss the process of negotiation to reaching an allocation decision nor do we analyze the process of allocating to each patient in detail.

The allocation rules discussed here ought not to be applied to allocating medical supplies to the treatment of life-threatening diseases or emergency treatment. There are more adequate allocation rules that account for these special cases such as application of prioritizing criteria e.g. triage in catastrophe situations.

The causes for shortages in medical allocation situations differ. They may stem from restricted financial resources (contribution fees, taxes etc.) to be distributed in the statutory health system or they adhere to naturally restricted medical supplies as in transplantation medicine where available organs are scarce. In this work we primarily focus on the problem of scarce financial resources.

Among different degrees of scarcity we have a common public finance situation in mind, in which not all public interests can be financed, yet each of them could be realized by itself. As we find this type of scarcity on different distribution levels, the model is easily applicable to situations in distributing tax revenues to different public interests as well as allocating a budget to departments in a hospital.

Concluding the introduction, this work combines the disciplines of cooperative bargaining theory and health economics with aspects of medicine, ethics and law.

2 Scarce resources in the German health system – an overview

2.1 Introduction to the German statutory system

In Germany two health systems coexist – a privately and a publicly organized system. While each citizen can be a member in the statutory German health system which is publicly financed and organized, a private health insurance is restricted with income. If income is equal or above the cap of 3,750 Euros monthly income in 2010 (which equals 45,000 Euros yearly income), people may choose between a privately or publicly funded health system. In fact, 83.3% (68.5 million) insured have no choice due to the income restriction and are statutory members in the publicly funded health system. Of those who have the choice 10.5% (8.6 million) are privately insured while only 4.6% (3.8 million) decide for the statutory system. [1]

Since this work is to show alternative methods in allocating medical resources we primarily focus on the statutory health system in Germany and give some basic information to understand the nature and functioning of that system. The German statutory health system is regulated by the fifth social security code (Fünftes Sozialgesetzbuch, abbr.: SGB V). According to the solidarity principle it aims to maintain, restore and improve the health state of all its insured members. Foremost we are interested in the allocation of medical resources such that we outline a scheme in figure 2.1 that reflects the path from collecting contributions to allocating medical services.

Centerpiece of the German statutory health system is the health fund, which was introduced in January of 2009. It functions as a pay-as-you-go financing institution which means that contributions to the system are used to finance all medical goods in the same period. It does not work according to the funding principle as you may expect from the notation of the institution. Most of the revenues to the health fund originally come from its members, their employers, and tax revenues. While both, employer and employee, contribute 14.6% of employee's salary, the employee bears an additional 0.9%.[2]

---

1   Bundesministerium für Gesundheit, Daten des Gesundheitswesens 2009, Tab.8.1.
2   Bundesministerium für Gesundheit, GKV-Beitragssatzverordnung vom 29.10.2008.

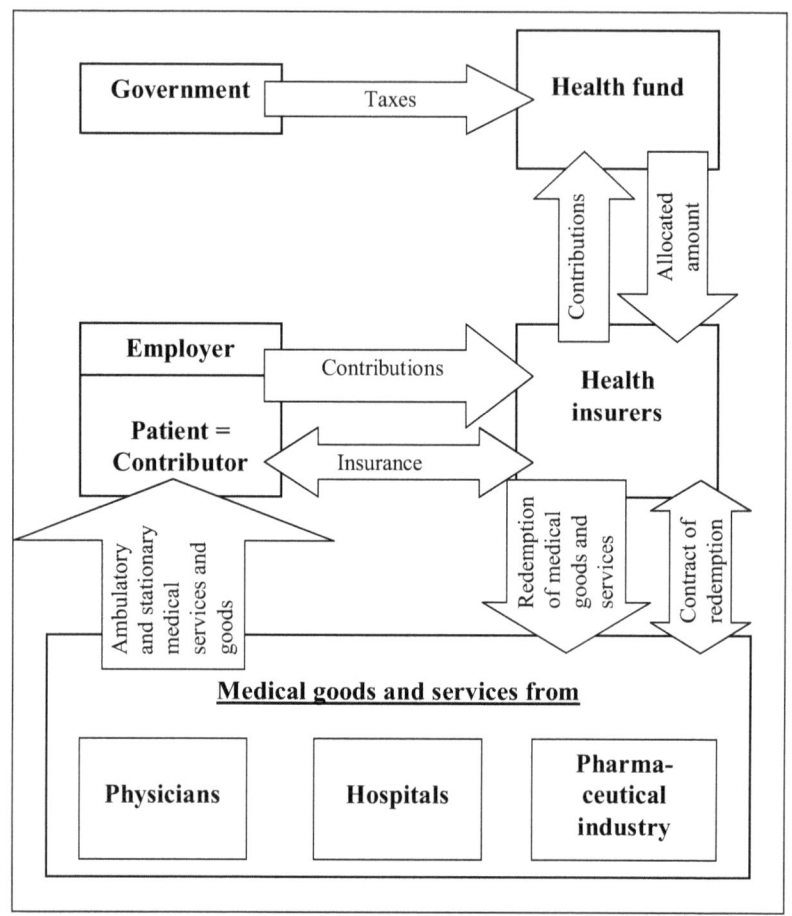

Figure 1.1: German statutory health system – an overview

In 2009 the health fund collected 164.51 billion Euros, (only 7.11 billion from tax revenues) and spent 166.99 billion Euros for medical goods and services and administrative costs. This leads to a deficit of 2.48 billion Euros in 2009.[3] Total collected contributions including tax revenues are reallocated to health insurers in a complex allocation mechanism. First, a basic amount which is assessed by average expenditures of the statutory health system is awarded to

---

3   Bundesministerium für Gesundheit, Gesetzliche Krankenversicherung vorläufige Rechnungsergebnisse 4. Quartal 2009.

each insured member. In the following classification process patients are grouped according to age and sex which determines either a premium or a rebate depending on their risk to use medical services. In detail young male patients receive a rebate on their basic amount whereas elder women receive a premium. In addition, the allocation depends on the type of disease of patients. On the basis of a morbidity filter 80 diseases are selected according to three main factors - chronic, fatal, and cost-intensive illness. In total, the allocation mechanism leads to different medical budgets transferred to each health insurer depending on the reallocation criteria. A macro budgeting process watches general finances and cost recovery in the health system. If the system is unbalanced, additional contributions or increasing contribution rates may result. For a more detailed introduction about the functioning of the health fund see Drabinski (2008).

In order to truly understand how the allocated amount of the health fund is finally redeemed to suppliers of medical goods and services, one has to comprise the organizational structure of health insurers, medical suppliers such as doctors, nurses, pharmacists etc. The national head organization of health insurers is the GKV-Spitzenverband that takes responsibility of 166 public health insurers[4] and is advising federal and national governments in medical issues. In addition, it is a voting member of the Federal Joint Committee (Gemeinsamer Bundesausschuss abbr.: G-BA), that is an institution that decides which treatment is to be included in the statutory treatment catalogue. In addition, this national organization together with the federal associations of health insurers (Landesverbände der Krankenkassen) contracts a master agreement with the association of physicians and hospitals in the statutory health system on federal and national level (Kassenärztliche Bundesvereinigung, Kassenärztliche Vereinigungen der Bundesländer, Deutsche Krankenhausgesellschaft, Landeskrankenhausgesellschaften). The master agreement constitutes terms and conditions of financial remuneration of medical services and goods rendered by physicians to patients according to statutory guidelines and previous treatments and become more concise on the federal contract level.

While contracting with physicians and hospitals proceeds with their corresponding associations, negotiating budgets for pharmaceuticals is limited.

---

4   GKV-Spitzenverband, Anzahl der Krankenkassen im Zeitablauf – Konzentrationsprozess durch Fusionen.

Besides Denmark and Malta, Germany is as of March 2010 the only European country with no price regulations for pharmaceuticals.[5] The prices for pharmaceuticals are fixed by the pharmaceutical producers, but health insurers may negotiate discount contracts on pharmaceuticals. Yet within the statutory health system a maximum redemption price for pharmaceutical impacts pricing strategies of the pharmaceutical industry.

The illustration of the distributive process in the German statutory health system shows that patients in the end receive medical goods and services from physicians, nurses, pharmacists, dentists ... . They are also financial contributor to the system in the form of contribution rates, additional payments, co-payments etc. In other words the distribution of financial resources in the German statutory health system proceeds on different levels. First, health expenditures compete with resources needed for other resorts such as education, environment, safety, and social benefits. Health resources are to be distributed within prevention, therapy, rehabilitation, technological progress, and medical education. Next lower level is the allocation of resources to patients groups, according to illness, or other social regional characteristics. On the lowest level medical resources are given to the individual patient.

For the years to come the German statutory health system faces two main challenges. First, the aging of its population leads prospectively to a shift in age cohorts such that a growing demand in services of elderly people stands face to face with a decreasing work force that contributes financially as well as provides medical services. According to the Federal Statistical Office (Statistisches Bundesamt (Eisenmenger et al. 2006)), the German population cohort of the 20 - 67 years-old shrinks until 2050 while the elderly population cohort of over 67 continues to grow. While the total population between 2005 and 2050 decreases from 82 million to 68 million, the percentage of 20-67 years old goes down from 63.3% to 54.4% and the fraction of people elder than 67 increases from 16.4% to 30.6% in the same period.[6] It is not hard to see that in the nearer future the pay-as-you go-principle for all social security services, not only the health system risks to run collapse. The phenomenon of an aging population is caused

---

5   GKV-Spitzenverband, So entstehen Arzneimittelpreise in der europäischen Union.
6   Eisenmenger et al. (2006), relevant data (p.57) are based on constant birth rate, life expectancy for men 83,5 and women 88.0 years in 2050 and negative migration balance.

by increasing life expectancy, decreasing birth rates, and negative external migration.

Second, increasing prices and utilization of medical goods and services stress financial stability of the German statutory health system. During 1999 and 2007 total expenditures in this system have climbed from 130.92 to 153.88 billion Euro which is an increase by 17,5%. Per capita spending in the same period has also climbed from 2,526 to 3,072 Euro which is an increase of 21.6%. Studying expenditure list of goods and services rendered, it strikes that the biggest increase occurs in pharmaceuticals (44.8% from 19.2 to 27.8 billion Euro between 1999-2007).[7] In 2008 the German federal institute for pharmaceuticals and medical products authorized 2160 new drugs, while 1880 permission discontinued.[8] A new drug which holds a patent presumably causes higher cost to the health system while it also gives higher benefit in treating patients. Studying the pharmaceutical index for 2008, the 30 largest revenue pharmaceuticals could possibly decrease costs by substituting medicine up to one billion Euro.[9]

In conclusion, we discussed two main aspects that heavily affect the pay-as-you-go-principle in the German statutory health system –demographic change and increasing medical costs.

In an ongoing political as well as scientific debate scientists and politicians are aware of scarce medical resources and certain institutions are in place to guide and govern.

First, the G-BA as mentioned earlier as the highest self-governing committee for physicians, dentists, psychotherapists, hospitals, and health insurers is responsible for regulating the treatment catalogue and constituting guidelines in quality management in the statutory health sector. It is connected with the institute of quality and efficacy in the German health system (Institut für Qualität und Wirtschaftlichkeit im Gesundheitswesen, abbr.: IQWiG)[10]. The IQWiG evaluates new treatment methods and gives advice if the proposed treatment method ought to be part of the treatment catalogue of the statutory health system or if an existing treatment is proven beneficial and ought to be

---

7   Bundesministerium für Gesundheit, Daten des Gesundheitswesens 2009.
8   Bundesinstitut für Arzneimittel und Medizinprodukte, Bearbeitungsstatistik: Zulassungs- und Registrierungsanträge.
9   Gesundheitsberichterstattung des Bundes, Einsparpotential der 30 umsatzstärksten Analogpräparate.
10   Institut für Wirtschaftlichkeit und Qualität im Gesundheitswesen.

included and vice versa. As a matter of fact, the IQWiG and its statement have an impact on the coverage of medical treatment in the statutory health system. For example under a new reimbursement rule new pharmaceuticals will be reimbursed when they prove a higher benefit than comparable products. In addition, the maximum price reimbursed depends on the additional benefit which means that reimbursements under the statutory system may not cover total medical cost. Therefore, the IQWiG's method of evaluating and assessing medical treatment are controversially discussed for example by the German ethics council. In a study of Ahlert/Kifmann (2009) acceptance of pricing on pharmaceutical was tested and it showed that the majority of people did not favor new regulations in medical reimbursements.

Second, the German ethics council which constitutes of 26 members from interdisciplinary backgrounds in science and politics, debates and publishes statements on socially important topics of the human sciences. In 2008 the council discussed the problem of resource allocation in the German statutory health system. Foremost, it criticized the methods of evaluating medical treatments as proposed by an institute for quality and cost-effectiveness in the health sector.[11]

Concluding this section of chapter 2 we have introduced important mechanisms and institutions in the German statutory health system and highlighted major challenges for the future. In the following paragraph we put emphasis on a well-known decision mechanism – bargaining. We discuss several examples and discuss situations in which a bargaining mechanism is already implemented in the health care system.

2.2 Examples of medical bargaining situations

There are two important aspects to the notion of bargaining – the process of finding a mutual agreement among opposing parties and the final bargaining outcome. Bargaining is an important conflict solving mechanism for various allocation problems in our society. We find bargaining situations throughout the health system quiet often – bargaining wages of physicians, bargaining the distribution key of health fund resources, health insurers bargain terms and conditions of services rendered with physicians, hospitals and pharmaceutical

---

11 Deutscher Ethikrat, Pressemitteilung 05/2008.

industry. Furthermore, physicians of different departments in a hospital bargain their budgets. In the following paragraphs we look at some examples more closely. As we study properties and solutions from cooperative bargaining, we focus on the outcome and the design of medical allocation mechanisms that impact the result.

First, bargaining wages is a very prominent application of the described allocation mechanism. In the medical sector wages of physicians, nurses and physical therapists etc. are negotiated. Several interest groups exist, such as the Marburger Bund that represents the interests employed and unemployed doctors, which may either be civil servants and state employees. In a press release of January 1st 2010 the Marburger Bund terminates collective wage agreements with the German Association of public employers (Vereinigung kommunaler Arbeitgeber abbr.: VKA). Marburger Bund requests an increase in salaries of five percent along with improving working conditions to combine family and career, as well as better compensation for on-call services. In the beginning of April 2010 negotiations fail to reach an agreement. Strike of medical employee or even threat of dismissal may follow if the parties won't come back and continue to reach an agreement.[12] The described process of wage negotiation is very common. Both parties present their offers which typically fall apart. If they are willing to concede they eventually reach an agreement.

Second, allocating financial resources from the health fund to public health insurers is a bargaining task. Earlier we introduced the German health fund and described that it pools contributions from employees, their employers and taxes which are redistributed to public health insurers in order to redeem medical goods and services. Especially, defining concise rules for this allocation mechanism requires an open and transparent process that resembles a negotiation. The process of establishing and adapting the structure of the health fund is lead by the German Insurance Federation (Bundesversicherungsamt abbr.: BVA). In fact the BVA and its designated board propose the classification of patient groups and disease but require cooperation from health insurers, medical suppliers and their corresponding institutions. In a hearing process for example relevant illnesses to be recognized are proposed to the BVA.[13] Participants may then bring forward why e.g. another disease ought to be

---

12   Marburger Bund, Tarifkonflikt Ärzte/VKA.
13   Bundesversicherungsamt, Festlegungen für das Ausgleichsjahr 2011.

included. Remarks will be recognized and revised. This type of negotiation is characterized by different powers of the negotiating parties. On the one hand, the BVA is leading the process of designing the allocation rules, yet encourages all participants in the health sector to comment and to propose.

Third, negotiations between KBV and GKV-Spitzenverband determine the remuneration of doctors in a negotiation process. A uniform value scale (einheitlicher Bewertungsmaßstab abbr.: EBM) is negotiated for medical treatments by a valuation committee (Bewertungsausschuss) which consists of members of KBV and GKV-Spitzenverband. Interestingly, if no consensus can be reached, a valuation committee that is expanded by usually three members (one independent and one for each party) is convened to come to a final decision. These decisions on national level bind local and federal public health insurers such as the BKK Landesverband. It is held liable for an agreement of redeeming extra-budgetary services such as radiation therapy or palliative care, new preventive care services such as Chlamydia screening, skin cancer screening and pediatric screening U7a. According to the annual report 2008 the increase in medical cost for additional services is not compensated by the increase in salaries and hence in contributions, higher contribution fees are expected.[14]

Fourth, negotiations about hospital budgets become more and more individualistic in contrast to other areas of the public health insurance system. While the BKK Landesverband for example is tied with agreements on doctor's fees on federal level, it may negotiate redemption fees with hospitals.[15] In order to be an equivalent negotiation party, health insurers need adequate qualifications in auditing, case management and controlling. The main purpose of the negotiation is fixing the budget with hospitals based on type and number of case-fees. The relevant basic case value for Hessen in 2010 accounts 2.968,56 Euro[16], which will be multiplied with the case mix index and the number of cases in a hospital. The case mix index is a sum of all diagnosis related groups weights in ration to the number of patients in a hospital. The determination of case mix index for German diagnosis related groups (G-DRG), the G-DRG-weights and the number of cases in G-DRG proceeds along the guidelines of the

---

14 BKK Landesverband Hessen, Geschäftsbericht 2008.
15 BKK Landesverband Hessen, Geschäftsbericht 2008.
16 Institut für das Entgeltsystem im Krankenhaus, Fallpauschalenkatalog 2010.

institute for hospital remuneration system (Institut für das Entgeltsystem im Krankenhaus abbr.: InEK).[17] The weights for example are assessed depending on the type of disease, its severity, age of patient and length of stay in hospital. In analogy to the redistribution of health fund resources, all participating partners may proposes changes to the classification of the G-DRG-classification which are considered by InEK. In addition, hospitals and health insurers may negotiate additional individual remuneration for services, such as hospital and nursing charges, vocational training, and specialized services of medical centers.

Fifth, since the health care reform in 2007, health insurers are encouraged to negotiate discounts on pharmaceuticals.[18] The scope of negotiating prices is restricted.[19] According to a study by IMS Health in 2009 59% of prescribed generics packages were under discount.[20] While of all discounted pharmaceuticals in 2009 96.4% were generics, only 1.3% were first-source pharmaceuticals and 0.7% were pharmaceuticals on patent.[21] AOK reports cost reduction in three-digit million Euros which equals 23% of medication revenues measured in pharmacy prices.[22] Pharmaceutical industry and health insurers usually keep secret about prospected savings in order to keep advantage in discount negotiation. As measured by total health expenditures the revealed magnitude of savings seems rather small. As prices are set by the pharmaceutical industry within legal pricing caps, health insurers can either negotiate individual active substances or substance group on off-patent pharmaceutical with selected suppliers. More complex are negotiations for on-patent pharmaceuticals which can be done by cost-sharing or risk-sharing agreements.

Sixth, we analyze the allocation of a hospital budget. Earlier we discussed how hospitals negotiate their budget with health insurers on the basis of case mix, number of treatments and case-fees. Each hospital is rewarded a budget to cover current medical costs such services to patients and in addition it is granted an investment budget through tax revenues. Investments to built a hospital and renew medical assets with a amortization time of 3 years and longer are publicly funded (Lüdeke/Allinger (2005)). While hospitals have to apply for grants on

---

17 Institut für das Entgeltsystem im Krankenhaus, Fallpauschalenkatalog 2010.
18 Bundesministerium für Gesundheit, Gesundheitsreform 2007 im Überblick.
19 Kassenärztliche Bundesvereinigung, Rabatte und Rabattverträge.
20 IMS Health, IMS Marktbericht.
21 Kassenärztliche Bundesvereinigung, Rabatte und Rabattverträge.
22 AOK Bundesverband, Rabattverträge 2009-2011.

investments, remuneration of current services are negotiated. Within a hospital current services are assessed depending on the remunerated case-fee (Keun/Prott (2008)). Case-fee allocation to medical departments in a hospital can be complicated when patients are treated in different departments (Ramme/Vetter (2002)). For example surgical intervention in a hospital may require a stay in the following departments: surgery, intensive care, rehabilitation. The case-fee will be allocated according to negotiated weight measures that account for length of stay and medical expenses in each department.

The previous examples from the German statutory health system showed that negotiations are an important tool to reach agreements in different situations and on different levels of the medical system. Yet there are many more issues that are negotiated, for example, the legal medical framework is an outcome of debates in the German Federal Parliament (Bundestag), the definition of the treatment catalogue, remuneration of dentists' and psychotherapists' services, wage negotiations for nurses and other medical staff, determining the tax revenues to the health system, determining the contribution fee and additional contributions… . In conclusion, we have discussed negotiations on different levels of the German statutory health system – on national, federal and individual level of physicians, health insurers, and pharmacists. We notice that the lower the level of negotiation the more concise become agreements and the more tied become negotiations on the next lower level.

Discussing medical bargaining situations each example represents a different aspect of bargaining. Restricted medical resources on the one side and claims of patients on the other makes parties negotiate. The parties have an original position and they express their expected claims. All parties will not be able to achieve this result due to the medical restriction. So parties have to be willing to give in and to concede in order to reach an agreement. We also find examples where the negotiation power of the parties is unequal which impacts the outcome. Foremost, the discussed examples of medical negotiation situations illustrate the process of negotiation and how to reach an agreement, but it is equally important to analyze the result to find out what allocation rule and which properties does the result characterize. Since negotiations are complex it is difficult to analyze their outcomes. This is a substantial part of this work and is discussed in a simple model throughout the following chapters.

2.3 Interdisciplinary discussion of scarce medical resources

After discussing facts and example situations in the German statutory health system, we give insight into the scientific discussion about scarce resources in medicine. We discuss interconnectedness of science, health sector, and political institutions. In addition, we introduce important notations and methods from health economics, and present result from research group FOR 655 "prioritizing in medicine" that are closely related to this topic.

2.3.1 Interconnectedness

In Germany we have an ongoing scientific discussion about scarce medical resources since the early 1990-ies. In the following paragraph we present examples how scientific research, medical sector, and political institutions are linked in the discussion of scarce resources in medicine.

Nagel and Fuchs (1993) published lectures of leading German scientists in medicine, ethics, economics, and law that were held on a symposium for "Social Justice in the Health Sector". Using the example of transplantation medicine in Germany scientists described the situation of scarce medical resources in organ allocation and scarce financial resources in the statutory health system and discussed alternatives to solve the conflict.

The central ethics commission (Zentrale Ethikkommission abbr.: ZEKO) is an institution that suggests a discussion about prioritizing criteria to face the problem of scarce medical resources in the German statutory health system in a statements of 2000^{23} and 2007^{24}. Originally founded by the German Medical Association (Bundesärztekammer), the ZEKO constitutes of 16 members from interdisciplinary scientific areas that strives to protect ethic principles in medicine. In 2007 it strengthens its request in establishing a prioritizing system to manage allocation of scarce financial resources in medicine.

An interdisciplinary discussion of scarce medical resources also takes place in the German ethics council (Deutscher Ethikrat) [25], the succeeding institution of the National ethics council, an institution that constitutes of

---

23 Zentrale Ethikkommission bei der Bundesärztekammer, 2000.
24 Zentrale Ethikkommission bei der Bundesärztekammer, 2007.
25 Deutscher Ethikrat, Pressemitteilung 05/2008.

interdisciplinary experts independent of politics who report regularly to the German parliament. Discussing scarce resources in the medical sector, they criticized evaluation methods of IQWiG for assessing medical treatments. In their opinion the applied method does not adhere to international standards and they demand that such important decisions need a broad interdisciplinary discussion.

Since 2007 the research group FOR 655 "Prioritizing in medicine" funded by the German Research Association (Deutsche Forschungsgemeinschaft, abbr.: DFG) discusses prioritization as an approach to problems of scarce resources in the German statutory health system.[26] The main project of the group is a survey on priority setting criteria in the German statutory system that will be conducted in representative sample of the German population (Diederich et al. 2009). Scientists from different areas such as medicine, psychology, philosophy, economics, and law discuss issues of priority setting in medicine with national and international scientists, politicians, and representatives from the medical sector.

In conclusion, the examples give an insight into the already deep anchored discussion of scarce medical resources in science in cooperation with medical sector and politics through different institutions. It becomes clear that we are aware of the problem of scarce medical resource and discuss solutions, although we are far from reaching a consensus of radically reforming the statutory health system in Germany. Especially the discussion in FOR 655 on priority setting which will be outlined later helped to bring forward this work.

2.3.2 Notations and Methods from health economics

For an overview of scientific approaches to scarce medical resources in health economics we give some basic economic definitions and methods translated into a medical context. Graf von der Schulenburg/Schöffski (1993) define three fundamentals that describe a basic medical allocation problem discussed in health economics. First, in the health sector we face allocation problems with scarce available resources confronted with very large claims of patients. Second, we find different allocation situations, and third we have patients with different needs. This encounter of medicine and economics is the challenge for

---

26 FOR 655 „Priorisierung in der Medizin" www.priorisierung-in-der-medizin.de.

establishing evaluation methods with the overall goal of allocating medical resources in the health sector to ensure economically efficient medical treatment suitable to patients' needs.

An economic approach to deal with restricted resources in the medical sector is to rationalize, to ration or to prioritize. According to Fuchs et al. (2009), rationalization in a medical context aims to increase efficiency and productivity in health service processes. A revision of medical processes is necessary in order to evaluate efficacy and alternatives to use economic reserves wisely. This means either to increase medical services with given financial resources or securing a medical standard with minimum financial resources.

Medical rationing in contrast to rationalization characterizes a situation in which necessary medical treatment is denied due to medical shortcomings. Such situations are caused by scarcity of resources either financially or medically. In organ allocation increasing financial resources cannot compensate a lack of available organs, whereas treatment capacities in intensive care are a based on an allocation decision in a hospital foremost due to a restricted financial budget. Prioritizing in medicine determines a ranking of certain criteria. Discussed criteria in a medical priority setting may be improvement of quality of life, success probabilities, age, contribution to welfare, profession, lifestyle, a.s.o. . We differentiate horizontal (between different medical areas) and vertical (diseases and their respective treatments within one medical area) priority setting. An application of prioritizing criteria leads to ranking lists which determines the order of treatments. Prioritizing does not automatically include a need to ration. Moreover it enables a weighing of treatments in order to determine their order. In connection with a reference value or a given financial budget it may well become a rationing instrument.

In the following we will explore three prominent methods which measure positive and negative effects of medical treatment by relating costs (in monetary units) and benefit (e.g. in medical or monetary units) of a treatment (Breyer et al.(2005)).

First, the method of cost-effectiveness analysis uses a one-dimensional scale and enables comparison of mutually exclusive treatments. As a result we receive hit lists medical treatments, yet treatments with different outcomes cannot be compared. The second method, which is cost-utility-analysis is a multidimensional concept that uses a health index such as QALYs (quality adjusted life years) to measure the benefit of a treatment. The assessment of QALYs considers changes in quality of life and length of life of a specific treatment on the basis of contingent valuation method and standard lottery. This method also allows to establish ranking lists of exclusive treatments but here we compare treatments with different medical effects. The first as well as the second method is less meaningful without a budget restriction or a reference value for medical treatments. Third, cost-benefit-analysis assesses benefits and cost of a treatment measured in monetary units. The approach of willingness to pay helps to assess costs for treatment effects. The method enables to evaluate a single treatment and to decide if a treatment ought to be conducted. The downturn is that the benefit of a measure is dependent on the individual willingness to pay, which may be higher for patients with higher income.

In conclusion, the evaluation methods have in common that they assess benefit and cost of a treatment. They differ in the way of measuring benefit of medical treatment. While the costs of treatment are comparatively easy to assess the benefit is much more difficult to determine. We illustrated three methods in measuring the benefit which are all criticized. In addition, the presented methods show the overall benefit yet we cannot conclude which patients benefit from a particular treatment.

The discussed methods how to deal with scarce medical resource do not compete with this approach of applying cooperative bargaining theory. Indeed it is part of an ensemble of measures to deal with scarce resources. Establishing efficient and effective medical processes and assessing ineffective treatments may be a pre-stage in dealing with scarce medical resources. As a result rationalization and cost-benefit-analysis should be a first approach to exclude ineffective treatments, before cooperative bargaining may be applied. While bargaining assigns shares of the budget to different patients groups, prioritizing criteria end resulting ranking lists may further allocate resources within these groups. Rationing comes in at any stage of resource allocation whenever the medical budget is too small to cover all treatments.

2.3.3 Results from FOR 655 „Prioritizing in medicine"

In 2007 an interdisciplinary group of German scientists from medicine, psychology, philosophy, law, and economics started to work on a project about priority setting in the German statutory health system. In a theoretical as well as an empirical approach guidelines in dealing with scarce financial resources and the need to prioritize in medicine are studied. Working papers and discussions in FOR 655 have inspired this work to a great extent. Therefore, we present some results that are important for the following chapters.

The theoretical and empirical work of the research group C4 within FOR 655 has been the major inspiration to this work. In the following we give insight into economic results on the definition of medical allocation problems and priority setting criteria as well as experimental studies.

First, we sum up some theoretical work. Ahlert (2005, 2006, 2007) define a medical allocation problem with thresholds in which patients have fixed needs. The problem is that the given medical budget does not suffice to satisfy all needs. In detail, Ahlert (2005) discusses priority ranking on the basis of different criteria such as decreasing and increasing in needed quantity, success probabilities as well as established rules such as first come first served and triage. Specific topics such as justified claims and the lexicographical combination of two or more criteria are considered and finally properties and priority rules such Rawlsian leximin criterion are discussed. Ahlert (2006) defines in addition to the allocation problem a random allocation rule, and presents solutions to the problem such as utilitarian ranking and equal chance allocation. Ahlert (2009) further discusses allocation of equal chances in medicine and defines the Equal Gain Rule.

The series of papers constitutes the underlying allocation problem for a bargaining model considered in this work. We loosen some of the assumption and introduce new parameters in this model.

Second, we explore some experimental scientific work in project C4 of FOR 655. In an experimental study Ahlert/Felder/Vogt (2008) investigate social preferences and choices of economists and physicians for treating patients compared to choices in neutrally framed allocation problems. Recipients differ in minimum needs and ability to profit. The authors classified distributors as selfish, rawlsian, utilitarian and maximizing of number allocated persons. Results showed that distributive norms go with different professional education. While medical students in the medical setting obeyed to their norms, economics students proofed economic norms in the neutral setting.

Kifmann/Ahlert (2009) studied general attitudes of members of the statutory health system towards cost-benefit-assessment for pharmaceuticals and determining upper limits in the statutory health system. What criteria are perceived as relevant in assessing the benefit of a medication? The data were provided by the spring questionnaire of Gesundheitsmonitor which is a sponsored research project by the Bertelsmann Stiftung. Analysis included descriptive statistics and multivariate analysis. The authors found that participants generally accept cost remuneration for medication, but are more likely to reject a statutory upper limit. A criterion of cost assessment is not accepted for remuneration of medication.

Ahlert et al. (2010) studied questions of allocation of medical resources to groups of different professional background (medicine, law, and economics). Medical (monetary) units are given to recipients with different minimal need and ability to benefit from the given resource. Classical justice concepts as well as variations due to threshold are studied. Results show that the professional education as well as the order of allocation problems mattered.

Concluding the theoretical and empirical work in this economic subproject in FOR 655, we state that major input for the model discussed in following chapters comes from this scientific research.

Beside the economic fundamentals, this work is inspired by other research groups from FOR 655.

Ahlert/Granigg/Greif-Higer/Kliemt/Otto (2008) present an allocation example from liver transplantation. Allocation mechanism for livers functions on the basis of the MELD score (model of end stage liver disease). Compared to kidney transplantation for which exists a substitution treatment (dialysis), transplantation of liver is without an effective alternative treatment. While we have established criteria in liver allocation it is unclear if it creates an increased number of deaths of patients on the waiting list due to postponing patients. The authors find that the number of instantaneous deaths may be smaller when patients awaiting a liver transplantation who have good success are not postponed until they become emergency cases. The authors consider an alternative allocation mechanism and a transitional period and discuss consequences.

Friedrich et al. (2009) propose a marginal efficiency criterion which functions as a posteriorization criterion. Treatments with low benefit, health-related quality of life, extension of life or other patient relevant criteria are cut off from the first round of allocation of resources. A common example is a treatment for a fatal disease that prolongs life for a few weeks. This raises the question of treatment standards at the end of life.

In medical law scientists comment judgments and decisions of courts and consider legal permission of changes for example the introduction of priority setting criteria such as age which means that the age of a patient may be a legitimate argument to refuse treatment. Huster (2005) discusses age rationing from view of different disciplines, for which he finds supporting and declining arguments. He justifies age as a rationing criterion since all patients eventually belong to the age cohort that suffers restricted treatment. Typically, we discuss the example of a patient elder than 70 who ought not to receive a hip joint replacement. On the other hand, we can also think of additional treatments for infants especially in premature care. After all, there is no need to reject age rationing when the allocation problem is conceived as a process to design a reliable allocation system for its members.

Dannecker et al. (2009) discuss the consequences of the Nikolaus decision to social, public and criminal law. For example, they discuss the legitimating of medical rationing in the health system. In 2005 the Nikolaus decision of the Federal Constitutional Court (Dec.6th, 2005, AZ1 BvR 347/98) ruled that public health insurers cannot refuse services in case of life-threatening diseases or an unavailability of a standard therapy or a chance of curing or positively influencing the course of the disease. This decision is applied in many following cases such as the Tomudex decision of the Federal Social Court (Bundessozialgericht) (Apr.4th, 2006 - B 1 KR 7/05 R - Tomudex®). As a consequence this decision may undermine financial restrictions in the German statutory health system. In addition, it also weakens decision making of the executive power.

Diederich et al. (2009) present a questionnaire on the determination of preferences over allocation of medical resources in the statutory health system. Stakeholder interviews as well as discussion among the research projects in FOR 655 generated a set of questions on different allocation situation in the statutory health system. Questions shall be presented to the participants in a representative survey. The study aims to find public perception of considering prioritizing criteria in allocating medical goods and services in the statutory health system. For example, the cost factor, when services according to the decision have to be finance by the statutory system.

2.3.4 A specific medical allocation problem

Philosophical literature constitutes a medical allocation problem that we use for this work. The well-known Taurek-example (Taurek (1977)) illustrates the allocation of a restricted medicine to either a group of five or a single person. We have two opposing groups: group one is a single person that needs the total amount of the available medicine, a second group contains five patients who each need one fifth of the available medicine. As a fact, the life-saving medicine can either save the life of one person or a group of five. The final allocation decision is deadly to the group that does not receive the medicine. The example raises lots of questions that are not completely answered. Does the number of people saved count? Are the lives assessed against each other? What difference does it make when we know the fate of one person? According to what rules shall we allocate medicine? Is it acceptable to toss a coin to come to a decision? The paper induces a controversial debate among philosophers and other scientists (Parfit (1978), Lübbe (2004), Ahlert/Kliemt (2008)).

The later discussed approach of cooperative bargaining is in so far similar to the Taurek example that our model uses two patient groups with predetermined medical claims and the available amount of medicine does not yield to treat both groups entirely. Yet the approaches differ in the assumption of division of resources. While Taurek constructs its examples such that either group can be saved we allow that some patients on both groups may receive some treatment. Also the assumption about deadly course of the disease if not treated is less dramatic. In addition, we allow partial treatment which leads to worse health state as if fully treated. Patients without treatment will not instantly die from illness, yet have a lower quality of live.

Summarizing this section, we gave an overview of major sources such as results from FOR 655 for this work, besides cooperative bargaining theory which we introduce next.

2.4 An introduction to cooperative bargaining theory

This part aims to provide underlying concepts and axioms for our model in the following chapters. In the following we introduce different academic fields that study bargaining. In addition, we present the Nash concept and two solution concepts – the Nash and Kalai/Smorodinsky bargaining concepts – from cooperative bargaining.

2.4.1 The notion of bargaining

Beside the application of cooperative bargaining in a medical context in this work, bargaining is a substantial part of our political, economical and private lives (Thomson (1994)). Beginning with a classification of bargaining in game theory, we shall outline some important findings that prove the close relationship of concepts from both lines. In addition, we give an outline of other disciplines that study bargaining in contrast to the cooperative game-theoretic approach in this work.

In 1950, when Nash's paper about the theoretic approach to bargaining was published, it opened doors to a large research field - game theory. In general, we distinct two directions of theoretical solution concepts – cooperative and non-cooperative game theory. While the non-cooperative approach focuses on the description of the person's moves (individual strategies) in order to reach an equilibrium outcome (strategy), cooperative bargaining theory, searches an outcome which fulfills certain desired properties (Eichberger (1993) and Binmore (1991)). Beside the work that has been done in the field of non-cooperative game theory, we will base our work on the grounds of cooperative game theory. Therefore, the main focus of this work is on solution concepts and their properties and not the process of reaching an agreement.

First, we outline the relationship of the famous Nash solution (Nash (1950)) to a microeconomic theory by Zeuthen (1930). While the Nash solution is one of the cooperative bargaining concepts studied later on, the Harsanyi-Zeuthen solution is a non cooperative approach to bargaining. Harsanyi (1956) proved that both solutions concepts under specific assumptions lead to identical solutions. The Nash solution is an axiomatized concept that encompasses Zeuthen's theory of wage negotiations (Zeuthen (1930)). The Zeuthen model is a procedural bargaining process in which two parties make alternating conceding offers until a mutually accepted solution is found. Each person may either accept the opponent's offer or stay with his own. The person that has the highest risk to threat a conflict is to make the next concession. Nash on the other hand, thought of a bargaining solution that fulfils desired properties and maximizes gains compared to the status quo.

Second, we illustrate a general version of the Nash solution, the non-symmetric Nash solution, that proves identical to another non-cooperative model from game theory - the Rubinstein model (Binmore et al. (1986)). This well-known strategic bargaining model was published by Rubinstein (1982), which involves two persons bargaining over the partition of a pie. Under an infinite time horizon both persons either accept or reject and make a counteroffer. In addition, each new round diminishes the net outcome due to bargaining cost and preferences over future and present settlements. If both persons are infinitely impatient and make counteroffers increasingly quickly, then the game is finished in the first round and each person receives half the pie. The more impatient person gives-in part of the pie, moreover, the first person is in advantage. The non-symmetric version of the Nash bargaining solution is presented by Kalai (1977) for two person bargaining problems. It is proven that the non-symmetric solution is the generalized Nash solution which fulfils three of the four proposed axioms by Nash (1950) except symmetry.

Third, a philosophical approach to bargaining by Gauthier (1986) proves consistent with an axiomatic approach by Kalai and Smorodinsky (1975), also studied in this work. After Luce and Raiffa (1957) criticized the Nash solution for the axiom of irrelevant alternatives, which in their argumentation are not irrelevant at all, Kalai and Smorodinsky published a different axiomatic approach that involves a monotonicity axiom. While the solution is well-defined for n-persons, the set of axioms is not identical with the original version of Kalai and Smorodinsky (1975). Roth (1979) showed that Pareto efficiency is not necessarily fulfilled when the solution concept is applied to a situation with more than 2 persons. Gauthier (1986) defines a philosophical theory over a bargaining process. While Nash postulates that persons compare their offers with status quo, Gauthier argues that persons keep in mind what they have requested and they compare it with the presented offer. So, the Gauthier bargaining concept describes a process in which persons make concession from the ideal offers. Gauthier and Kalai/Smorodinsky solutions are identical (Roemer (1998)).

Fourth, in experimental game theory has become popular for testing theoretic concepts. Cooperative bargaining concepts are studied in forms of ultimatum games (Kagel and Roth (1997)). In an ultimatum game typically two persons interact in sharing a sum of money. Persons will receive compensation after the game that may depend on the solution. The simplest form of an ultimatum game is played by a proposer and a responder, whereby the proposer offers how to share a sum of given experimental currency and the responder either accepts or rejects. In the first case the sum is split according to the proposal in the second case both persons receive nothing. According to game-theoretic solution concepts, any positive amount is accepted by the responder. Knowing that, the proposer shall offer the smallest possible partition to the responder and the remainder is for him. This strategy leads to a subgame perfect Nash equilibrium, yet experimental studies have shown that a substantial amount of small offers have been rejected by the responder (Güth et al. (1982)). Nydegger and Owen present in an experimental study that some of the axioms of the Nash solution do not hold. In another allocation experiment Yaari and Bar Hillel (1984) prove that Nash and Kalai/Smorodinsky solution concepts do not necessarily predict behavior in realistic allocation situation. Klemisch-Ahlert (1996) studied recorded bargaining experiments and found that persons have aspiration levels in mind which they want to meet.

Fifth, we find many scientific sources that deal with allocation rules, their solutions and properties as well as aspects of fair distribution of resources which is strongly related to cooperative bargaining. Young (1995) proposes individual solution mechanisms. There is not a single mechanism for all the different allocation problems in the world. Child custody, kidney allocation, divide-and-chose problems need specific allocation mechanisms that address an initial problem. He discusses problems of divisible goods and offers solution mechanisms such as lottery, queuing, priority list, and bargaining. Brams/Taylor (1996) write on criteria and properties of fair division and define notions of fairness and presents allocation rules on cake division examples investigating envy-freeness. Moulin (2004) determines principles of fair distribution (compensation, reward, fitness...) and studies properties of allocation rules on the fair division of resources and on population monotonicity. Last, Ostrom

(1990) designs institution mechanisms for common-pool resources e.g. regulating fishing, restoring fishing grounds and keeping fisher's existence. She proposes self-enforcing rules that need no governmental control.

Last, we present a scientific line that studies negotiation techniques. A more business-oriented guide to bargaining is the Harvard negotiation project by Fisher und Ury (1981) which concentrates on the procedural course of a negotiation situation. The heart of the program is finding win-win-situations in negotiations such that both parties feel they have gained through bargaining. Raiffa et al. (2002) present an approach to analyzing negotiations. Beside the Harvard concept, Thompson (2005) publishes another guide to negotiations. One aspect in negotiating is that the bargaining parties need to pay close attention to reach an efficient outcome. Efficiency, here, focuses on the allocation of resources without leftovers. The bargaining process shall not waste resources and find an agreement which exploits both parties' interests. This is an interesting aspect that we also discuss within our cooperative bargaining models.

In economic literature we often read the term negotiation instead of bargaining. Stevens (1958) gives a distinction between both. Bargaining is an exchange transaction with minimum information exchange on the terms of trade. Negotiating further involves information exchange on a transaction. Since we will focus on the actual exchange we prefer to use the term bargaining and may use negotiation where it seems appropriate.

So far, we gave an overview of different academic fields of studying bargaining that are related to our work.

2.4.2 The Nash concept

Throughout the following paragraphs we present basic notations and definitions from cooperative bargaining and introduce properties as well as two bargaining concepts - the Nash and the Kalai/Smorodinsky solutions. We begin with a characterization of cooperative bargaining according to Nash (1950). Besides Nash, Roth (1979) and Thomson (1994) give an introduction to the Nash bargaining concept.

In every bargaining situation we find n-persons who we assume behave rational and are equal in their bargaining skills. Each one knows about its own as well as the others' preferences and desires. We determine a group of persons D with $i = \{1,...,n\}$.

In the literature we find several interchangeable notations for "person" such as party, participant or player, yet we may stick to "person". A person either bargains herself or has an agent who acts on her behalf. We assume that they have rational preferences and meet rational decisions. The persons have expectations about the solution, they determine feasible alternatives z that establish a bargaining set S which is compact and convex[27] and it holds that each $z \in S$.

We model the assessment of feasible alternatives z in S on the basis of utility theory. Feasible alternatives are shifted into utility space so that we receive a utility pair for each alternative that assigns a certain benefit to each person. The preferences over alternatives are embedded in a cardinal utility function of the form $u_i(z) = z_i$ with $\forall i \in D$ and $\forall z \in S$.

Applying a cardinal utility function, a person may differentiate among various alternatives, rank them from best to worst, and in addition, may measure how much better an alternative is compared to another. Yet experimental results show that utility concepts do not necessarily project the exact benefit of a person from an alternative. Kahnemann and Tversky (1979) found in their study that people tend to overestimate small and underestimate large probabilities. Although we base our model on utility theory we will later see that the presented solution concepts and their outcome are independent of utility measurement over feasible alternatives.

In cooperative bargaining we typically refer to two prominent alternatives – the status quo d and the ideal point $\overline{X}$. The original position of a person is called a status quo. When the person fails to come to an agreement they threat to be left with the status quo. The ideal point, on the other hand, is an alternative that combines the original requests of several persons. Let us start to bargain from that allocation in the plane where the persons claim the maximum outputs in the individual rational set of S. This is the *ideal point* of a bargaining situation $\overline{X}(S,d)$ which is defined by $\overline{x_i} = \max\{z_i | (z_1, z_2) \geq d, (z_1, z_2) \notin S\}$ with $i=1,...,n$. The ideal point is typically not a feasible alternative, while the status quo is such

---

27 Convexity and compactness characterize a set. If all segments in a line are part of the set, it is called convex. If a set is bounded and its boundaries are part of the set we say it is compact.

that $d \in S$ and $\overline{X} \notin S$ hold. Depending on the cooperative bargaining concepts discussed later on, a solution alternative is compared to either reference point.

A bargaining situation or bargaining problem (S, d) is characterized by a bargaining set S and a status quo d. The class of feasible bargaining situation for n persons in positive n-dimensional space R^{n+} is called B^{n+}.

A bargaining solution to a given bargaining situation is a mapping f of the bargaining situation (S,d) to a real-valued function $f(S,d)$ with $f(S,d) \in S$ $\forall (S,d) \in B^{n+}$.

In order to motivate rational persons to participate in bargaining they ought to have an incentive. If a solution to a bargaining situation $f(S,d)$ yields a better outcome for each person compared to the status quo d then we assume that the persons have an incentive to bargain such that $f(S,d) > d$. When the status quo is equal to the origin the bargaining situation is $(S,0)$ as illustrated in figure 2.2.

2.4.3 The Nash bargaining solution

After introducing the Nash bargaining concept we present the well-known Nash bargaining solution. Nash's solution concept is based on a set of axioms representing desired qualities of a bargaining solution. When all parties agree on the solution according to Nash, it has the properties of invariance under positive affine transformation of the utility function, weak Pareto optimality, symmetry and, independence of irrelevant alternatives.

Axiom INV (Invariance of positive affine transformation of the utility function): A bargaining situation $(S,d) \in B^{n+}$ and real numbers $\alpha_1,...\alpha_n > 0$ and $\beta_1,...\beta_n$ are characterized by a bargaining situation $(S',0)$ such that:
$S' = \{z \in R^{n+} | \exists z \in S : z_i = \alpha_i z_i + \beta_i \forall i\}$ and $d_i = \alpha_i z_i + \beta_i$
then $f_i(S',d') = \alpha_i f_i(S,d) + \beta_i$ with $i=1,..., n$.

Each person applies its own utility transformation on the set of alternatives. A positive affine transformation does not affect the solution. This aspect is illustrated in figure 2.3. Different transformation functions mean, that we cannot compare the persons' utilities. As a positive affine transformation of the utility functions does not impact a solution, we may bargain over the original units of the assets.

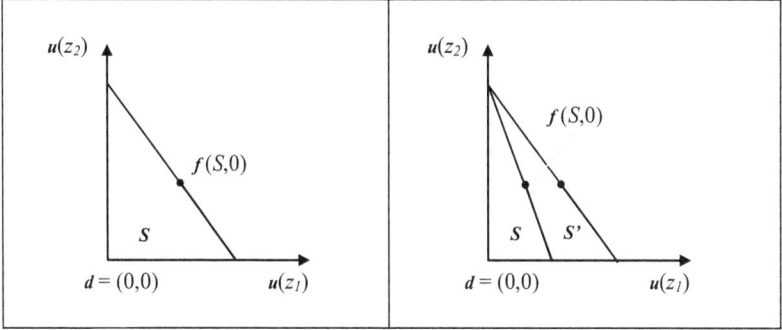

Figure 2.1: A bargaining situation

Figure 2.2: Property of invariance of positive affine transformation

Axiom WPO (Weak Pareto Optimality): If we have a bargaining situation $(S,0) \in B^{n+}$ and elements $z, z' \in S$ with $z > z'$ (componentwise) then $f(S,0) \neq z'$.

Consider a solution to a bargaining problem to be $f(S,0)$. If we cannot find another point in S where all persons are better off, then $f(S,0)$ is a weakly Pareto optimal solution to the bargaining situation. Figure 2.4 illustrates two feasible solution alternatives under the property of WPO.

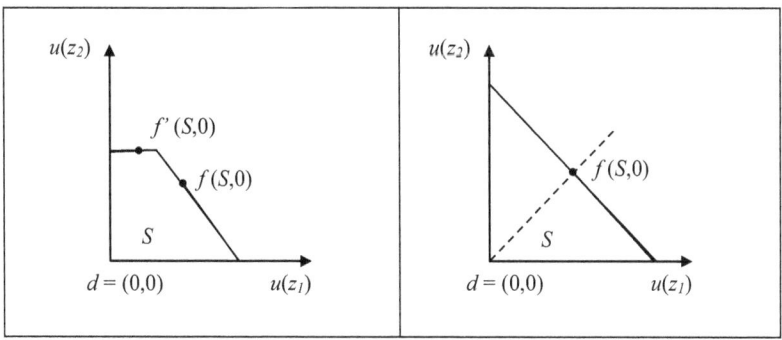

Figure 2.3: Property of weak Pareto optimality

Figure 2.4: Property of symmetry

47

Axiom SYM (Symmetry): Let (S,d) be a symmetric bargaining situation from B^{n+} with $d_1 = d_2 = ... = d_n$ and z as well as all permutations of z are in S, then $f_1(S,d) = f_2(S,d) = ... = f_n(S,d)$.

A symmetric bargaining situation does not distinguish between persons. Accordingly, the solution to a bargaining problem shall not distinguish between them either. If a bargaining situation assigns symmetric roles to the persons, it is common sense that they receive an equal pay-off as shown in Figure 2.5.

Axiom IRR (Independence of irrelevant alternatives): Let $(S,0)$ and $(S',0) \in B^{n+}$ be bargaining situations with $S \subset S'$ and $f(S',0) \in S$, then $f(S,0) = f(S',0)$.

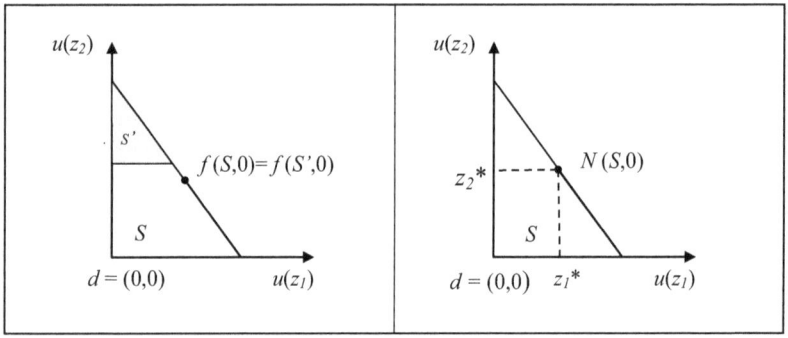

Figure 2.5: Property of independence of irrelevant of alternatives

Figure 2.6: The Nash solution $N(S,0)$

If an alternative is considered irrelevant the outcome ought to be independent of it. That means irrelevant alternatives do not affect the solution. Figure 2.6 shows bargaining situations with identical status quo that differ in so far that certain alternatives are no longer available in the subset. Yet these situations ought to yield the same outcome as long as the solution is still available in the subset.

The four presented properties uniquely define the Nash bargaining solution.

Theorem 2.1: The Nash Solution $N(S,0)$ is the only bargaining solution to fulfill the axioms of INV, WPO, SYM, and IRR on B^{n+}.

The proof shall be omitted. The interested reader may study Thomson (1994).

The Nash solution is a bargaining solution which compared to the status quo maximizes the product over gains in the individual rational space. In figure 2.7 we see a triangular bargaining situation which is a special case in that the Nash solution is equal to the midpoint of the hypotenuses.

2.4.4 The Kalai/Smorodinsky bargaining solution for two groups of patients ($n = 2$)

The following solution concept was introduced by Kalai and Smorodinsky (1975) and refers to critique of Luce and Raiffa (1957) on Nash's theory especially about the property of irrelevant alternatives. Let us consider two bargaining situations from figure 2.6 $(S',0)$ and $(S,0)$ such that $S \subset S'$. So the subset S is derived by eliminating the gray-shaded area in bargaining situation S'. According to Nash, the solution is the same in both situations as long as the outcome $f(S',0)$ is still available in the subset. Luce and Raiffa (1957), on the contrary, argue that the Nash solution neglects that person 2 gives up some of her feasible alternatives. Compared to person 1 person 2 looses part of her bargaining power towards reaching an agreement. Then the solution ought to reflect that certain alternatives are no longer attractive to person 2 which means the solution outcome for person two decreases.

Kalai and Smorodinsky (1975) introduce their solution concept on the grounds of three of Nash's axioms. They substitute the axiom of independence of irrelevant alternatives with a monotonicity requirement. The basic idea of the Kalai/Smorodinsky solution is that the solution reacts to changes in the bargaining situations such that it requires equal relative concession of each person compared to their initial requests.

Axiom RMON (Restricted Monotonicity): We have two sets $(S,0)$ and $(S',0)$ with $S \subset S'$ and $\overline{X}(S',0) = \overline{X}(S,0)$. Then for the solution it holds that $f(S',d) \geq f(S,d)$.

Figure 2.8 shows how the bargaining solution changes when a bargaining situation changes. If all persons cannot reach their ideal point then they all have to reduce their requests equally.

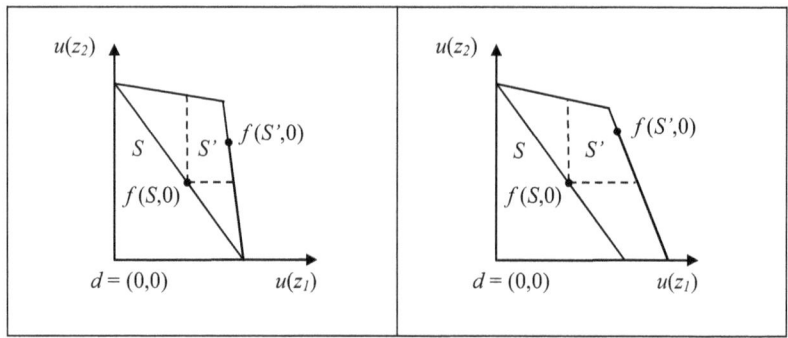

Figure 2.7: Property of restricted monotonicity

Figure 2.8: Property of individual monotonicity

Axiom IMON (Individual Monotonicity): We have two sets $(S,0)$ and $(S',0)$ with $S \subset S'$ and $\overline{X}(S',0) \geq \overline{X}(S,0)$ with $i=1,\ldots,n$ such that it holds $\overline{x}_k(S',0) > \overline{x}_k(S,0)$ for one k in D and $\overline{x}_i(S',0) = \overline{x}_i(S,0)$ for all other i not k. Then for the solutions it holds that $f(S',d) \geq f(S,d)$.

The described property is similar to the property of restricted monotonicity. It simply differs in the condition where monotonicity holds. IMON is illustrated in figure 2.9.

Theorem 2.2: The Kalai/Smorodinsky solution $\mu(S,0)$ is the only solution in B^{2+} to satisfy the axioms INV, SYM, WPO and RMON.

For a proof of theorem 2.2 see Kalai and Smorodinsky (1975).

The solution is unique in terms of deriving a result of relative equal concessions compared to the ideal point. In other words, the persons agree on a solution which assigns the same proportional share of their original requests which is $(z_1 - d_1)/(\overline{x}_1 - d_1) = (z_2 - d_2)/(\overline{x}_2 - d_2)$. In figure 2.10 shows the Kalai/

Smorodinsky solution which geometrically is the maximal point on the line $\overline{dX}$ that is still an element of S.

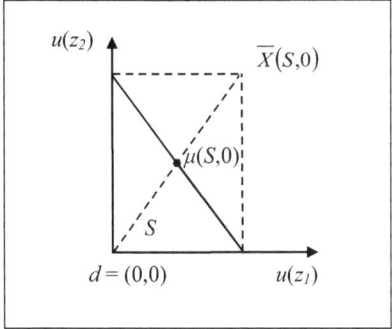

Figure 2.9: The Kalai/Smorodinsky bargaining solution

As Roth (1979) shows for bargaining with 3 or more persons, theorem 1.2 holds only for the two-person-case. It turns out that weak Pareto optimality may not be fulfilled. Roth's impossibility result (Roth (1979)) shows that the set of desired of properties of the Kalai/Smorodinsky solution is not transferable to a larger group of persons.

2.4.5 The Kalai/Smorodinsky bargaining solution for more than two groups of patients (n > 2)

Thomson/Lensberg (1989) define the Kalai/Smorodinsky solution for more than 2 persons. An important element of that characterization is the property of population monotonicity which expresses a form of solidarity when a new person enters the situation. The claim of that new person is regarded as legitimate as everyone else's and causes greater reductions to all old persons. All persons ought to share according to the new group size. If a solution fulfils this property then it is population monotonic.

We have two bargaining sets S which contains of a group $V = 1,2$ and S' containing $W = 1,2,3$. The problem is such that we may compare what person 1 gets in S to what she gets in T. The same is true for person 2. The problem S with V is equivalent to the projection of S' from R^W to R^V which we call S'^V and it means that the arrival of a new person does not cause external effects.

For a definition of the Kalai/Smorodinsky solution we require the following axioms (Thomson/Lensberg (1989)). Only comprehensive sets are considered which means we allow free disposal of utility.

Anonymity (AN): For all $V, V' \in \wp$ with $|V| = |V'|$, for all mappings $\gamma: V \to V'$, for all $S \in B^{V+}$, for all $S' \in B^{V+}$, if $S' = \{z' \in R^{V'} | \exists z \in S \, s.t. \forall i \in V, z'_{\gamma(i)} = z_i\}$, then for all $i \in V$, $f_{\gamma(i)}(S') = f_i(S)$.

The property says that two groups of the same size solve two bargaining problems with identical structure in the same way. The names of the persons are not important. The relevant information to solve the problem is inherited in the problem itself not the persons involved. AN is a generalized property of SYM.

Continuity (CONT): For all $V \in \Lambda$, for all sequences $\{S^\lambda\} \subset B^{V+}$ converging in the Hausdorff topology to some $S \in B^{V+}$, $f(S^\lambda) \to f(S)$.

The property requires that small changes in the bargaining problem lead to small changes in the solution outcome.

Population monotonicity (POMON): For all $V, W \in \Lambda$ with $V \subset W$, for all $S \in B^{V+}$, for all $S' \in B^{W+}$, if $S = S'^V$, then $f(S) \geq f(S'^V)$.

As discussed in the beginning of this section the property describes that none of the persons should be better off after a new person is recognized.

The properties of WPO and SINV which are part of theorem 2.3 shall not further be discussed. Their content is identical to an earlier definition and the appropriate versions of these axioms can be studied in Thomson/Lensberg (1989).

Theorem 2.3: The Kalai/Smorodinsky solution satisfies WPO, SINV, AN, CONT and POMON.

The proof can be studied in Thomson/Lensberg (1989).#

So far we have given an basic overview of cooperative bargaining theory as we apply it to a medical allocation problem. Especially the aspect that these concept not only represent allocation rules but also demonstrate important criteria in distributing resource and hence in distributional justice, motivates an application in the health care issues.

At the end of the second chapter we notice broad framework of this work, as we discussed the statutory health care system in Germany, gave examples of negotiation in the health system, illustrated the interdisciplinary and multi-institutional approach to discussing scarce medical resources in Germany. Most importantly, we summarized interesting results of the DFG-funded research group FOR 655 and introduced the theoretical structure of the model in the following chapters. To be clear, this work is not meant to influence political decision making, it discusses properties and solutions to a specific medical allocation problem.

3 A cooperative bargaining model for two groups of patients

3.1 Introduction

The model in this chapter refers to a medical allocation problem that has been discussed in philosophic literature since the late 70ies of the 20th century. In detail, the Parfit-Taurek discussion (e.g. in Lübbe (2004)) is about Taurek's example of saving the lives of 5 individuals versus the life of 1 with the same amount of medicine. This illustrates a dilemma situation in allocating medical resources to patients. Ahlert (2006) generalizes Taurek's example in health economics and defines an allocation problem with a finite number of patients who each have an individual need. The total amount of the medical good does not suffice to fulfill all needs. This chapter considers this type of models and defines and analyzes solutions to such allocation situations. We apply cooperative bargaining theory and characterize allocation mechanisms by their normative properties.

Finding solutions to the described allocation problem one may consider different solution concepts. First, we may apply a stochastic process that chooses patients with a certain probability. Ahlert (2006) and Ahlert (2009) define such a random mechanism for the allocation problem. A second approach considers allocating medical resources according to a priority list as proposed by Ahlert (2005) and Zimmermann (2009). Finally, we contribute to the discussion by applying a cooperative bargaining approach to the allocation problem. That is, we model the allocation problem as a bargaining problem and we claim normative axioms for a solution that are derived from cooperative bargaining theory. In particular, we focus on the bargaining concepts of Nash (1950) and Kalai/Smorodinsky (1975).

We discuss an allocation problem for a perfectly divisible good that is to be allocated to two groups of patients. Each group has an individual claim towards that good. If that group receives the requested amount it gains a higher health state than if not given the amount. The total amount available to share is not enough to serve all patients in all groups. We consider this allocation problem in the context of cooperative bargaining theory and show that for two representative patients we have a unique solution that satisfies the axioms symmetry, weak Pareto optimality and invariance under positive affine transformation. We show that the solution is equal to the Nash and the Kalai/Smorodinsky solution. The allocation mechanism assigns equal chances to receive the requested amounts, which we interpret as receiving half the medical budget.

The chapter is organized as follows. In section 1.2 we define assumptions and notations of the model such as a chance of receiving a medical good and success probabilities under the condition of treatment or no treatment. In section 1.3 we introduce a cooperative bargaining problem for two groups with one patient in each group. We model a set of chances of success which we denote the bargaining set and define a status quo in bargaining, a bargaining problem, and solution. Section 1.4 discusses the axioms of symmetry, weak Pareto optimality and invariance under positive affine transformation. We show that there exists a unique solution that satisfies the three axioms. Furthermore, we proof that the solution is equal to the Nash and the Kalai/Smorodinsky solution. Finally, we summarize the results and give implications for further research in section 1.5.

3.2 Definition of an allocation problem

The situation in the model represents a situation in health economics. One can think of the process of allocating medical resources to departments in a hospital or to resorts of national health care services.

Patients are modeled in patients groups which are understood as their assigned diagnosis-treatment-pairs. Patients in one group have similar diagnosis and treatment related characteristics such as illness, treatment catalogue and success probabilities in case of being treated or in case of not being treated. As a result, we assume that patients in one group are homogenous in these characteristics and heterogeneous compared to other groups. Each group may be headed by a representative that acts on behalf of the patients in that group. This person has perfect knowledge of the type of illness and possible treatments for patients in that group. For example, dialysis patients are treated in one department of a hospital. These patients' interests (medical claims) are represented by the head of department which is typically an experienced doctor. By assumption this person knows the medically indicated needs of dialysis patients treated in his department and the expected number of patients per time unit considered. He claims a portion of the budget equal to sum of these requests.

For this paper we introduce a model for two patients groups i with $i = 1,2$ and each group has one representative patient. Off course, the model can be generalized to more than two diagnosis-treatment pairs and to more than one patient in each group. As we assume to have only one patient in each group we may simplify notations. When we use the notation of group i we refer to the representative patient of that group.

We denote by q the amount of money that pays for a certain supply of medical goods and services. The amount of medical supplies q is considered perfectly divisible. For example, a hospital is assigned a fixed amount of money annually, which restricts the number of medical services of the hospital in that year. The amount of medical resources can be interpreted in monetary units. However, we use the term medical resources and medical treatment in relation to the medical allocation problem and keep in mind that medical resources, of course, are financed by a monetary budget.

We denote by q_i the amount of medicine of the representative person of group i. For the representative patient in each group we are given a medical need q_i towards the medical resource. The amount each patient may request is determined by medical guidelines or treatment catalogue such as medical goods and services are predetermined in the German statutory health system. The claim entitles patients to a certain type of treatment. The patient must receive this amount, since giving more or less is a waste of resource and considered a futile allocation as defined by Ahlert (2006).

The allocation problem is such that the total amount of medical supply available is not enough to fulfill the requests of both groups, though each single claim could be realized within the given budget. Therefore, the restriction is such that $\sum_{i=1,2} q_i > q$.

For the patient in each group we are given success probabilities. We call the success probability for a representative patient i with treatment s_i and the success probability without treatment r_i. A probability of success without treatment characterizes the health state and the quality of life of that person for a given period of time, when the patient does not receive the requested good. A probability of success with treatment, on the other hand characterizes the health state and the quality of life of that person for the given period, if the patient receives treatment. We simplify the complexity of the increase of health by assuming that health status can be represented by one dimensional parameter, the probability to become "healthy". We assume that receiving treatment significantly increases the health state and the quality of life of the person for some time compared to a situation when no treatment is given. There are situations, e.g. in palliative care, when one cannot increase patients' health state significantly yet this patient is still treated. Nonetheless we focus on situations in which we can significantly increase patient's health levels. We assume that any medical treatment will increase the quality of life for that individual such that $0 \leq r_i < s_i \leq 1$. Success probabilities are determined by an experienced doctor, for example, who is able to estimate average quality of life for a patient treated in his department when this patient receives or does not receive treatment.

For two groups with one representative patient each a vector $s = (s_1, s_2)$ represents the probabilities of success with treatment and $r = (r_1, r_2)$ represents the probabilities of success without treatment such that $r < s$, componentwise, i. $r_1 < s_1$ and $r_2 < s_2$.

We define an allocation problem a for two groups with one patient in each group, the individual needs of these patients q_i and their success probabilities with and without treatment s_i and r_i according to Ahlert (2006) such that $a = (q; q_1; q_2; r_1; r_2; s_1; s_2)$. The set of all allocation problems for two groups is denoted by A_2.

For the allocation problem a we determine feasible deterministic allocations for a given supply of medical goods and individual needs. A feasible deterministic allocation is a vector $x = (x_1, x_2)$ such that $x_i \in \{0,1\}$ and $\sum_{i=1,2} x_i q_i \leq q$. Since we do not consider futile allocations, only two situations become available. First, $x_i = 1$ what means that patient i receives its requested amount and patient $j \neq i$ does not, i.e. $x_j = 0$. Second, $x_i = 0$ that means patient i receives nothing and patient $j \neq i$ receives the needed amount, i.e. $x_j = 1$. Each feasible deterministic allocation x represents an allocation where one patient receives the requested amount of the medical good and the other does not. In addition, of course, the allocation where nobody is treated is feasible, too. The set of all feasible deterministic allocations x of an allocation problem $a \in A_2$ is denoted by F. By allowing lotteries on the set of deterministic feasible allocations we will enlarge the set of feasible allocations such that we will construct a feasible set of allocations that is the convex closure of F.

3.2.1 An example

Consider the situation $q = 10$, $n = 2$, $q_1 = 3$, $q_2 = 9$. This is an example of two groups with only one patient in each group which is illustrated in figure 3.1. Feasible deterministic allocations of the example are $(0,0)$, $(1,0)$, and $(0,1)$. Efficient allocations are $(1,0)$ and $(0,1)$ such that only one of the two patients receives the requested amount.

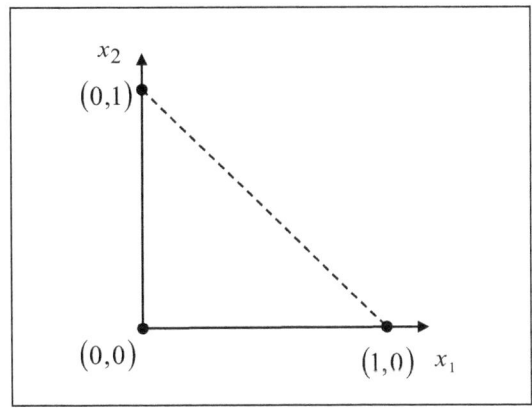

Figure 3.1: Feasible deterministic allocations for an allocation problem with
$$q = 10, \ n = 2, \ q_1 = 3, \ q_2 = 9$$

The given allocation problem a generates deterministic allocations such that each allocation $x \in F$ could help one of two patients. In allocation situations in which we cannot help all, we may demand that each legitimate claim is considered in the allocation process. Each patient with a specified claim that could in principle be satisfied ought to have a chance to receive the medical good under the allocation mechanism.

Ahlert (2006) defines a random allocation mechanism over feasible deterministic allocations. This generates chances of receiving the requested amount. A random allocation for a given allocation problem $a \in A_2$ assigns a probability distribution on the set of feasible deterministic allocations F and a random allocation rule h applied to a chooses a probability distribution $h(a) = p$ on F. The set P contains of all probability distributions p on F.

We consider the set of feasible deterministic allocations F of an allocation problem a and a probability distribution p on F which chooses a feasible deterministic allocation $x \in F$ with $p(x)$.

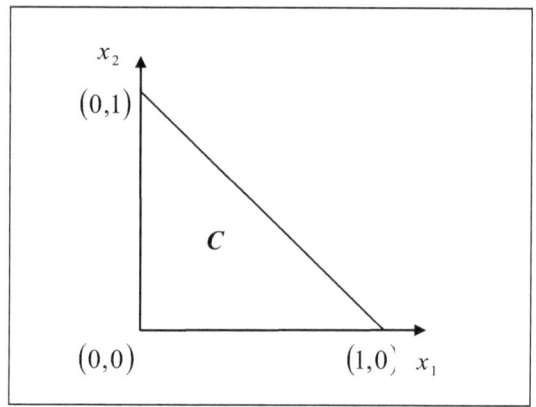

Figure 3.2: A set of feasible chance allocations

For a given probability distribution p on F we denote by $c_i(p)$ the chance that patient i receives the good. The chance that she receives the good is the sum of probabilities over all chances of feasible allocations with $x_i = 1$ such that $c_i(p) = \sum_{x \in F} x_i p(x)$. For the chance to receive the good $0 \le c_i(p) \le 1$ holds.

The vector $c = (c_1(p), c_2(p))$ for a given P then represents a feasible chance allocation for two patients. C denotes the set of all feasible chance allocations. Each vector $c \in C$ is originated by some probability distribution p on F. The set C is generated by the set of all lotteries over feasible deterministic allocations and is represented by the convex closure of F (Ahlert 2006). For the introduced example from Ahlert (2006), the chance allocation problem is shown in figure 3.2.

In addition to a chance of receiving the good $c_i(p)$, we denote the chance of not receiving the good by $\overline{c_i}(p)$. Then a chance of not receiving the good is $\overline{c_i}(p) = 1 - c_i(p)$.

Before we define chances of success, we need to refine the definition of probabilities of success with and without treatment. We understand a probability of success with treatment s_i to be a chance of success (E) under the condition of being treated (D).

A conditional chance of success s_i if patient i is treated is defined by
$$s_i = P(E|D) = P(E \cap D)/P(D) = s_i \cdot c_i(p)/c_i(p).$$

We understand a probability of success without treatment r_i to be a chance of success (E) under the condition on not being treated ($\overline{D}$).

A conditional chance of success r_i if patient i is not treated is defined by
$$r_i = P(E/\overline{D}) = P(E \cap \overline{D})/P(\overline{D}) = r_i \cdot (1 - c_i(p))/(1 - c_i(p)).$$

According to our definition, a chance of success for the patient in group i is the combined probability of chances of success with and without treatment. The probability of success l_i is such that
$$l_i = P(E) = P(E \cap \overline{D}) + P(E \cap D) = s_i \cdot c_i(p) + r_i \cdot (1 - c_i(p)).$$

Rearranging the above equation, we derive $l_i = c_i(p) \cdot (s_i - r_i) + r_i$. Under the assumption that probabilities r_i and s_i are given, a chance of success is a positive affine transformation of chances of receiving treatment. The term $(s_i - r_i)$ represents the gain in chances of success when a patient receives treatment. By definition it holds that $0 < (s_i - r_i) < 1$. A group receives a positive increase in chances of success when she is allocated. A one percent increase in chances of receiving treatment results in an increase in chances of success by $(s_i - r_i)$ percent.

A chance of success for the patient in group i determines an expected living quality as indicated by the health state of that group. The expected health state of that patient depends on his success probabilities and whether or not she is treated. A patient's success probability indicates chances to recover from an illness in a given period of time.

3.2.2 A cooperative bargaining problem of chances of success

In the following, we give an introduction to notations from cooperative game theory (Roth (1979) and Thomson (1994)).

We define a set of allocations of chances of success for two groups with one patient in each group. We start with the deterministic allocations: each feasible deterministic allocation $x \in F$ can be represented by a chance vector of receiving the good such that the components $c_i(p) \in \{0,1\}$ for at most one $i = 1,2$. We can further determine a chance of success $l_i = c_i(p)*(s_i - r_i) + r_i$ for such values of $c_i(p)$. For each chance of receiving the good $c_i(p) = 1$ we generate a chance of success $l_i = s_i$ and for $c_i(p) = 0$ we receive $l_i = r_i$. We call y a feasible chance allocation of success with $y = (y_1, y_2)$ and $y_i = \{r_i, s_i\}$ with $i = 1,2$. For each $x \in F$ we derive a chance vector y. The set of all chance vectors y generated from deterministic feasible allocations is called G. For the given allocation problem, feasible allocations of chances of success in G are $\{(r_1, r_2);(r_1, s_2);(s_1, r_2)\}$.

We consider a set of feasible chance allocations of success G of an allocation problem a and a probability distribution p' on G which chooses a chance allocation of success $y \in G$ with $p'(y)$. The set P' contains all probability distributions p' on G.

A vector $l = (l_1(p'), l_2(p'))$ for a given distribution p' on G represents a feasible chance allocation of success for two patients. A set L is the set of all feasible chance allocations for chances of success. Each vector $l \in L$ is originated by a probability distribution p' on G. A set L is determined by a lottery over feasible deterministic allocations y with a probability distribution p' on G. And L is a convex closure of G like C was the convex closure of F (Ahlert (2006)). We understand a set L to be a *bargaining set* in a cooperative bargaining model.

The chance of success for patients in group i is the sum of probabilities over all feasible allocations such that $l_i(p') = \sum_{y \in G} y_i p'(y)$. The chance of success $l_i(p')$ for group i is such that $0 \leq r_i \leq l_i \leq s_i \leq 1$ under the restriction that $r_i < s_i$. When no patient receives treatment, i.e. $c_i(p) = 0$, all realize an expected health state $l_i = r_i$ for $i = 1,2$. That is the situation when no representative is treated is denoted by r. Given a set L, we call this allocation the status quo or *original health state* $r = (r_1, r_2)$. From the definition of L we know that $r \in L$.

When both groups are treated with certainty, we arrive at $l = s$. We understand the vector $s = (s_1, s_2)$ as the vector of best possible health states that all patients can attain in case they all would receive treatment. From the definition of feasible chances of success for an allocation problem a we conclude that s is not a feasible chance vector in the set of feasible chances of success L such that $s \notin L$. This is obvious because treating all individuals of all groups is impossible under the definition of the allocation problem a. We call this vector s the *ideal health state* of all patients which refers to the notation of ideal point in cooperative bargaining theory.

The set L as discussed is the convex hull of the allocations of chances of success $\{(r_1, r_2); (r_1, s_2); (s_1, r_2); (s_1, s_2)\}$. Depending on the type of the allocation problem a we may have different types of sets of possible chances of success L.

First, a feasible set is for example derived by a situation when no patient receives treatment. Then we arrive at $L = \{(r_1, r_2)\}$. Second, we receive two more sets of chances of success when the situation is such that we can help either one group or the other. In case we help group 1 we have a set of chances of success that is the convex hull of the following chance allocations such that $L = ch\{(r_1, r_2); (s_1, r_2)\}$. On the other hand, it is possible that only group 2 receives treatment. Then the set of chances of success is such that $L = ch\{(r_1, r_2); (r_1, s_2)\}$. Neither of the discussed sets of allocation of chances is referred to in this chapter, since they do not impose an allocation situation in that respect that two groups compete about scarce medical resources.

We focus on feasible set of chances of success $L = ch\{(r_1, r_2); (r_1, s_2); (s_1, r_2)\}$ as illustrated in figure 3.3. We receive such a set when all representative patients have the chance to improve their health status, i.e. under the given allocation problem it is feasible to treat them.

For the allocation situation we assume that there exists an $l \in L$ such that $l > r$ (componentwise such that $l_i > r_i$ for $i = 1,2$), i.e. each representative has an *individual rational incentive* to bargain. If we admit only patients that have a chance to improve their expected health status compared to the status quo, then representative patients have an incentive to agree to the application of this allocation mechanism. As a result, representatives whose needs are greater than the total amount of medical resource cannot be treated and are excluded from the allocation as well as representatives with no significant increases in success probabilities with treatment.

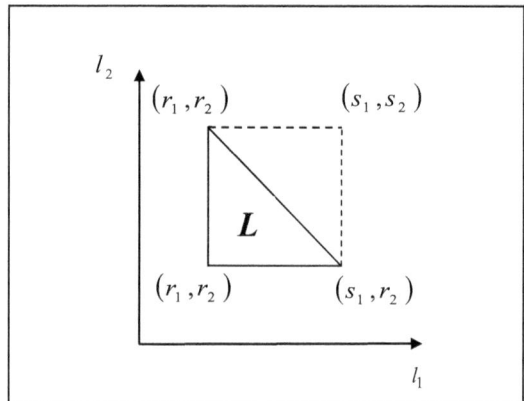

Figure 3.3: A set of feasible chances of success

Due to the definition of individual rationality, we restrict feasible sets of chances of success to sets $L = ch\{(r_1, r_2); (r_1, s_2); (s_1, r_2)\}$ as illustrated in figure 3.3. Since we have defined a chance of success l_i for $i = 1, 2$ in the interval $[0,1]$, each set L is a triangle situation and such sets form a restricted positive two-dimensional space which we denote by $\widetilde{R}^{2+}$.

A pair (L, r) with $L \in \widetilde{R}^{2+}$ and $r \in L$ is called a *bargaining problem*, if there is at least one $l \in L$ such that $l > r$.

We denote the class of all bargaining problems for two representative patients constructed as described above by $\widetilde{B}^{2+}$. The class of bargaining problems $\widetilde{B}^{2+}$ considered in this paper contains all triangular problems (L, r) with chance set $L \in \widetilde{R}^{2+}$ and $r \in L$. The class $\widetilde{B}^{2+}$ considered in this chapter is a restricted domain of bargaining problems. Due to restrictions of chances of success l_i the class $\tilde{B}^{2+}$ contains fewer problems than the unrestricted class of bargaining problems B^{2+} for two persons in cooperative bargaining theory.

A function $f: \tilde{B}^{2+} \to \tilde{R}^{2+}$ such that for every $(L,r) \in \tilde{B}^{2+}$ $f(L,r) \in L$ is a *bargaining solution* on $\tilde{B}^2$.

We interpret the solution of the bargaining problem as an allocation of expected chances of success that represents an expected health state for each representative patient. For a given allocation problem the solution to the bargaining problem is a consequence of a social agreement on desired properties such that the allocation mechanism determines an expected health state for each group.

3.3 Axiomatic characterization and solution concepts

We model desired properties of an allocation rule in the framework of cooperative bargaining theory and define solution concepts that fulfill these properties.

Since $\tilde{B}^{2+}$ consists of different triangular situations with status quo at the origin of the rectangle we have to model how the allocation should react on changes in the status quo or in the gain of success of each patient. We will assume that the representatives do not make interpersonal comparisons of the probabilities. That means if e.g. r_1 and s_1 change by some positive affine transformation this should not affect the allocation to patient 2 and vice versa. This implies that the allocation to patient 1 is changed according to his or her transformation. Allowing positive affine transformations for both patients lead to the axiom of invariance known from cooperative bargaining without interpersonal comparisons of utilities.

We consider a bargaining problem (L,r) from $\tilde{B}^{2+}$ with success probabilities r_i and s_i for each patient and assume that these probabilities shift to $\tilde{r}_i$ and $\tilde{s}_i$ for $i = 1,2$ such that we receive a vector of individual shifts for all patients $\tilde{r}$ and $\tilde{s}$. Then the corresponding chances of success l_i shift to $\tilde{l}_i$ for $i = 1,2$. For each allocation of chances of success $l \in L$ we receive a chance allocation $\tilde{l}$. A set of chances of success for the new situation is called $\tilde{L}$ such that all $\tilde{l} \in \tilde{L}$.

Axiom S.INV (Invariance under positive affine transformation of success probabilities): Given a bargaining problem $(L,r) \in \tilde{B}^{2+}$ and new probabilities of success $\tilde{r}_i$ and $\tilde{s}_i$ with $0 \leq \tilde{r}_i < \tilde{s}_i \leq 1$ let the bargaining problem $(\tilde{L},\tilde{r})$ be defined by

$$\tilde{L} = \{\tilde{l} \in \tilde{R}^{2+} \mid \exists l \in L \text{ such that } \tilde{l}_i = (\tilde{s}_i - \tilde{r}_i) \cdot l_i + \tilde{r}_i \text{ for } i = 1,2\}.$$

Then $f_i(\tilde{L},\tilde{r}) = (\tilde{s}_i - \tilde{r}_i) \cdot f_i(L,r) + \tilde{r}_i$ for $i = 1,2$.

A solution to the bargaining problem shifts analogously to the vector of individual shifts of probabilities of success of the representative patients. This axiom in the last consequence implies that every situation is equivalent to the triangle $\text{ch}\{(0,0),(0,1),(1,0)\}$. That means that the medical allocation problem is independent of the values of r_i and s_i.

Axiom S.WPO (Weak Pareto optimality in allocation of chances of success): Given any $(L,r) \in \tilde{B}^{2+}$. If $l \in L$ and there exists another chance allocation $k \in L$ such that $l' > l$ holds (componentwise: $l'_i > l_i$ for $i = 1,2$), then $l \neq f(L,r)$.

The axiom is a well known and socially desirable requirement for allocations also used in bargaining theory. Weak Pareto optimality is desirable because it requires a solution to the bargaining problem such that one cannot achieve better health states for both groups simultaneously. It may be possible to improve the health states for one group with the other group remaining at the same level. SWPO implies that a solution to the bargaining problem is situated on the weak Pareto optimal border of the chance set (which is in the cases considered here identical to the set of strongly Pareto optimal allocations) which is visualized as a bold line in figure 3.4.

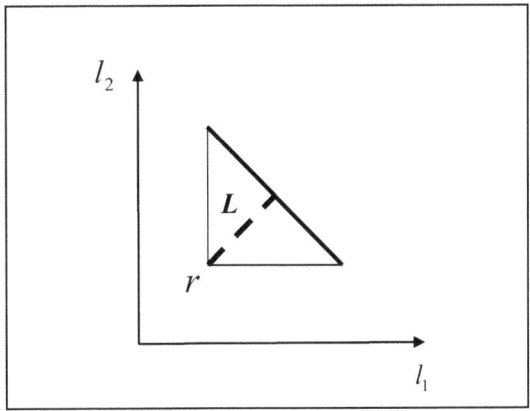

Figure 3.4: Weak (=strong) Pareto efficient set and symmetric alternatives

Axiom S.SYM (Symmetry in chances of success): Let (L,r) be a symmetric bargaining problem in $\widetilde{B}^{2+}$ ($r_1 = r_2$ and $s_1 = s_2$), i.e. for each $l \in L$ every permutation of l is also in L. Then $f_1(L,r) = f_2(L,r)$.

This property is a translation of symmetry from cooperative bargaining theory. If we have a symmetric bargaining problem, we cannot distinguish between representatives with respect to their success probabilities and chances to receive treatment. Yet groups may differ in the type of illness, however, this information is not included in the representation of the bargaining problem. The axiom requires that the solution to the problem is also symmetric. In our model a symmetric solution assigns equal expected increase of health states compared to the status quo to both groups. A solution to a symmetric bargaining problem must be an allocation on the dashed line in figure 3.4.

In the following we give a definition of two solution concepts from cooperative bargaining of two-person problems on the unrestricted domain of bargaining problems in B^{2+}. In chapter 2 we gave an overview of the Nash and the Kalai/Smorodinsky solutions.

First, we introduce the Nash solution which is uniquely defined three discussed axioms and independence of irrelevant alternatives (IRR). We defined the first three for bargaining problems on $\widetilde{B}^{2+}$ and they are reductions of the general axioms and it is known from literature (e.g. Thomson (1994)) that these axioms apply to B^{2+}. The Axiom of independence of irrelevant alternatives states that a solution to a bargaining problem does not change when certain feasible alternative are no longer available under a new problem. This holds only under the condition that the status quo in both situations is identical and the solutions are feasible alternatives in the old and the new situation. As we study triangular situations this axiom becomes obsolete.

Second, we define the Kalai/Smorodinsky solution which is characterized on B^{2+} by the axioms of invariance under positive affine transformations, weak Pareto optimality, symmetry and restricted monotonicity (RMON). Again, the first three axioms are reductions of general axioms on B^{2+} (Roth(1979)). The axiom states that a solution in two different bargaining situations that do not differ in their ideal points and status quos a solution to the larger bargaining problem is at least as big as in the smaller problem. Since we study triangular situations this axiom becomes obsolete.

Both solution concepts fulfill the axioms of INV, WPO, and SYM on B^{2+}. For any triangular situation on B^{2+} these three axioms define a unique solution. We use INV to shift the original problem to a symmetric bargaining problem. Applying SYM and WPO to this problem leads to a unique solution. The only solution with equal coordinates that is weakly Pareto optimal must be the midpoint of the hypotenuses of the triangular situation. The results of the general class hold on any subclass of B^{2+}. The restricted domain of bargaining problems $\widetilde{B}^{2+}$ considered in this paper is a subclass of bargaining problems in B^{2+} such that $\widetilde{B}^{2+} \subseteq B^{2+}$. Then for any bargaining problem (L,r) in B^{2+}, we receive an analogous result.

Theorem 3.1: There is a unique bargaining solution on the class of bargaining problems $\widetilde{B}^{2+}$ that satisfies the axioms of S.INV, S.WPO, and S.SYM. This solution is equivalent to the Nash and the Kalai/Smorodinsky solution on $\widetilde{B}^{2+}$.

The proof proceeds in three steps. First, we show that the required properties imply the uniqueness of the solution on $\widetilde{B}^{2+}$. Second, we show that this solution is equal to the Nash and Kalai/Smorodinsky solution. Third, we show that the unique solution fulfils the three axioms.

Proof. We consider any bargaining problem (L,r) from the class of problems $\widetilde{B}^{2+}$. By S.INV we may construct a bargaining problem (L',r') such that $r'=(0,0)$ and $L'=ch\{(0,0);(0,1);(1,0)\}$ (Compare figure 3.5). The bargaining problem is symmetric. A solution to a symmetric bargaining problem is an allocation in L' with equal coordinates for $i=1,2$. We construct a set of symmetric allocations L^{SYM} such that $L^{SYM}=ch\{(0,0);(1,1)\}$. We denote the set of weakly Pareto optimal allocations in L' with L^{WPO} such that $L^{WPO}=ch\{(0,1);(1,0)\}$. The intersection of the weakly Pareto optimal set and the symmetric set $L^{SYM} \cap L^{WPO}$ gives us allocations of equal coordinates that are weakly Pareto optimal. The only weakly Pareto optimal allocation wit equal coordinates is determined by a lottery on L^{WPO} which assigns each deterministic allocation a probability of ½. Therefore, $L^{SYM} \cap L^{WPO} = \{(1/2,1/2)\}$. It follows that $f(L',0)=(1/2,1/2)$. By S.INV we may transform the solution of the situation $(L',0)$ into any other solution of a bargaining problem (L,r) within $\widetilde{B}^{2+}$. This shows that the unique solution always chooses the midpoint of the hypotenuse for situations in $\widetilde{B}^{2+}$. This completes the first part of the proof.

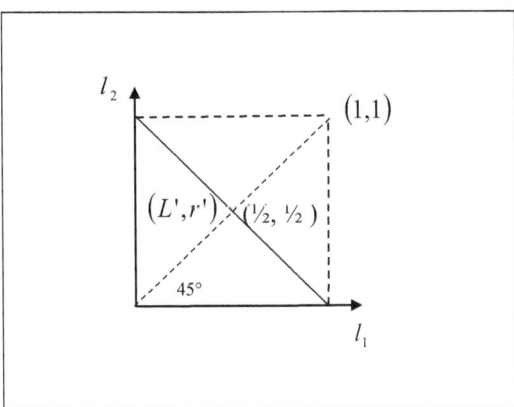

Figure 3.5: Bargaining problem (L',r') for $n=2$.

Next, we show that the unique solution is equal to the Nash and Kalai/Smorodinsky solution restricted to $\widetilde{B}^{2+}$. It is known from the literature and easy to see from the properties of the Nash and Kalai/Smorodinsky solution that

69

applied to triangle situations with status quo in the rectangle they both pick the midpoint of the hypotenuse as the solution. This means that any solution on $\widetilde{B}^{2+}$ fulfilling the three axioms is identical to the Nash and to the Kalai/Smorodinsky solution.

The third part is to recall that the Nash and the Kalai/Smorodinsky solution fulfill the axioms of symmetry and weak Pareto optimality on the set B^{2+} of all bargaining situations with two parties and therefore especially fulfill these properties on $\widetilde{B}^{2+}$. The axiom of invariance under positive affine transformations in our context allows less positive affine transformations than the general axiom for bargaining solutions on B^{2+} since translations are restricted not to exceed the interval [0,1]. Since the Nash and the Kalai/Smorodinsky solution both fulfill the stronger requirement on B^{2+} they also fulfill the weaker requirement on the smaller domain $\widetilde{B}^{2+}$. Thus the solution function f on $\widetilde{B}^{2+}$ fulfils the axioms of S.INV, S.SYM, and S.WPO.

This completes the proof.

3.4 Results and Conclusion

We apply bargaining theory to the simple case of two groups with one patient in each group. By assumption these two patients are representatives for patients in their groups. Here, the bargaining concepts of Nash and Kalai/Smorodinsky lead to the same unique solution. Each patient receives treatment with the probability of ½ such that a patient realizes equal (proportional) expected gains in health states compared to the status quo. This is equivalent to equal (proportional) expected decreases in health states compared to the ideal health states. In this case the solution concepts of Nash and Kalai/Smorodinsky represent a special egalitarian principle. By S.INV we may discuss the solution not only as an allocation of chances to receive treatment, but as receiving an allocation of the budget. In the definition of the allocation problem we are given a budget that exceeds the sum of claims of all groups. Interpreting the solution accordingly, each group receives half the budget. This interpretation does not further specify the allocation within each group.

On the set of the considered two-person cases the above solution mechanism can be uniquely characterized by the properties of weak Pareto efficiency, symmetry, and invariance under positive affine transformations. In the special case of bargaining situations considered here the concepts of weak and strong Pareto optimality lead to the same allocations. According to strong Pareto efficiency, expected health states of the solution allocation cannot be improved individually without decreasing another patient's health state. The property of symmetry requires that identical conditions in the allocation problem lead to identical allocations of expected health states under the solution concept. Transformation invariance refers to applicable positive affine transformations of success probabilities of each patient individually. The stochastic solution is independent of such positive affine transformations of individual success probabilities.

Further research on situations with two patient groups with different group sizes is planned. This must be done in another model which allows different numbers of basically homogenous types of individuals in each group together with their needs. Then we can again analyze the situation by applying cooperative bargaining theory. It is obvious that on this space the concepts of Nash and Kalai/Smorodinsky lead to different solutions. In the following chapter both solutions are characterized by normative properties in this space.

4 A cooperative bargaining model with two patients groups, their individual needs and different group size

4.1 Introduction

The model in this chapter is an adapted version of the model in the previous chapter. Again, we draw upon a dilemma situation in allocating medical resources to patients. The well-known Parfit-Taurek discussion (e.g. in Lübbe (2004)) is about saving the life of 5 individuals versus the life of 1 with the same amount of medicine. Ahlert (2009) and generalizes Taurek's example in health economics and defines an allocation problem with a finite number of patients who each have an individual need. The total amount of the medical good does not suffice to fulfill all needs. This chapter considers this type of model and defines and analyzes solutions to such allocation situations. In analogy to the previous chapter we apply cooperative bargaining theory and characterize allocation mechanisms by their normative properties.

Finding solutions to the described allocation problem, one may consider different solution concepts. Ahlert (2006) and Ahlert (2009) define a random solution mechanism for such an allocation problem. A second approach considers allocating medical resources according to a priority list as proposed by Ahlert (2005) and Zimmermann (2009). Finally, we continue the discussion from the previous chapter by applying a cooperative bargaining approach to the allocation problem. In contrast to the first paper, we now consider a model with two groups and that each has more than one patient. In addition, we model a situation of distributing medical resources to patients while disregarding success probabilities. In analogy, we model an allocation problem as a bargaining problem and we claim normative axioms for a solution that are derived from cooperative bargaining theory. In particular, we focus on the bargaining concepts of Nash (1950) and Kalai/Smorodinsky (1975) that yield different solutions that we discuss in detail.

We discuss an allocation problem for a perfectly divisible medical good for two patients groups with different group size. The groups are characterized by their individual medical claims toward standard treatment. The given medical budget is to be allocated to two groups of different size under the restriction that not all patients may receive standard treatment. We apply cooperate bargaining theory to the problem and show that for the case of two groups the Nash and the Kalai/Smorodinsky solution yield different solutions on a restricted domain. The solution concept of Nash assigns equal budgets to both groups regardless of group size as long as sharing the budget equally is efficient under the given allocation problem. On the other hand, the solution concept of Kalai/Smorodinsky assigns equal relative budgets depending on the maximum number of patients that can be treated in each group. We discuss both concepts in their application of sharing medical resources.

The chapter is organized as follows. In section 2 we define a two-group-model with its necessary notations and assumptions. Then in section 3 we define a cooperative bargaining problem for two groups and different group size. In section 4 we present two solution concepts from cooperative bargaining theory – the Nash and the Kalai/Smorodinsky solution. Section 5 sums up with a discussion of the results as well as implications from the bargaining theory for distributing medical resources and further comments.

4.2 The model

The situation in the model may represent a situation of allocating medical resources to resorts of national health care services which can be departments in a hospital.

Patients in the model are categorized in two diagnosis-treatment pairs which we call groups. Patients in one group have similar diagnosis and treatment related characteristics such as illness, treatment catalogue and success probabilities in case of being treated or in case of not being treated. As a result, we assume that patients in one group are homogenous in these characteristics and heterogeneous compared to other groups. So we have two groups $i = 1,2$ of any size n_1, $n_2 > 0$. The sum of patients in both groups is $\sum_{i=1,2} n_i$. The set of patients in group 1 and 2 are called I and J respectively. The required quantity q_i for a patient in group i is predetermined by medical guidelines that recommend a certain type of treatment for each disease. We call the medical amount that is necessary to sufficiently cure a patient standard treatment. Each patient under a statutory health system ought to claim this medical treatment.

Each group has a representative that claims the needs of the patients in that group. This person may be an experienced doctor and we assume that she has perfect knowledge of the type of illness and desirable and necessary treatments for patients in that group. The claim of one group is equal to the sum of claims of all patients in the represented group. Then the total requested quantity equals $\sum_{i=1,2} n_i q_i$. In a hospital for example the responsible of a department claims an amount that covers expected cost, i.e. she knows the estimate number of patients to be treated in the following period and she knows the cost per treatment.

For the two groups we are given a *medical budget* q. The budget can be interpreted as medical supplies and services for patients in either group or money that can be spend on such. The medical budget is perfectly divisible. The allocation situation is such that the budget does not suffice to fulfill standard claims of all groups together such that $\sum_{i=1,2} q_i n_i > q$. Though in fact there is enough to cover the claims of each group individually such that $q_i n_i \leq q$ for $i = 1,2$. In real allocation problems, and not only in medicine we typically have a situations when medical resources suffice to cover single projects, yet as a matter of lack of resources not all may be supported completely.

We define an *allocation problem* $a = (q; q_1; q_2; n_1; n_2)$ with $0 < q_i \leq q$ for $i = 1,2$, $q, q_i, n_i \in R^+$. The set of all allocation problems for two groups is called A_2.

For a given allocation problem, allocations that meet the required conditions are called feasible. It is a two dimensional vector of integer numbers that state how many individuals in each group receive standard treatment.

For a given allocation problem $a = (q; q_1; q_2; n_1; n_2)$ with two groups a *feasible vector* of treatable patients is $x = (x_1, x_2)$ with $x_i \in \{0,1,...,n_i\}$, $i = 1,2$, such that $\sum_{i=1,2} x_i q_i \leq q$. In the following we may call the vector x a feasible vector of patients sets *F(a)* and mean a feasible allocation that assigns treatment to a number of patients in each group under the given allocation problem. Then the sum of $\sum_{i=1,2} x_i q_i$ represents the amount of medical resources requested by patients in both groups. If $x_i = 0$ then none in group i receives treatment. For $x_i \in \{0,1,...,n_i\}$ the respective number of patients in that group receives treatment. Though the number of patients that receive medicine is determined, it is not clear which patients in that group receive the medical good. $F(a)$ is the set of all feasible number pairs $x = (x_1, x_2)$ of an allocation problem $a = (q; q_1; q_2; n_1; n_2)$.

Among feasible allocations there are number pairs such that the amount of the budget that remains after the allocation does not suffice to allocate to another patient in any group. Ahlert (2009) calls such an allocation strongly Pareto efficient allocation.

Before distributing medical resources each group anticipates the outcome of that process which we interpret as the best result that is feasible under the given medical budget. Each doctor hopes to be able to give treatment to all expected patients. The maximum number of patients that can be treated is dependent on the maximum number of treatment a group may realize if the entire medical budget is allocated to one group.

Given a medical budget q, the *maximum number of patients* that can be treated in each group is a vector $\overline{n} = (\overline{n_1}, \overline{n_2})$ such that $\overline{n_i}$ is the maximal natural number such that $\overline{n_i} \leq q/q_i$ for $i = 1, 2$. Then the maximum budget allocation for each group is a vector $\overline{q} = (\overline{q_1}, \overline{q_2})$ such that $\overline{q_i} = \min\{q, q_i \overline{n_i}\}$ for $i = 1, 2$. Under the given allocation problem a the vectors $\overline{n}$ and $\overline{q}$ respectively cannot be realized for both groups simultaneously.

Despite the fact that the medical budget is sufficient to fulfill each individual claim of a group, in all deterministic and discrete allocations in F we have a situation that we cannot treat all patients in all groups. It is desirable in such a situation that we consider all feasible deterministic vectors of patients sets. In a similar approach Ahlert (2009) proposes to use a random allocation rule to deal with positive chances. Here we use a random allocation mechanism over feasible vectors of patient sets which then determine vectors of expected numbers of treatable patients for each group. A doctor typically knows on average how many patients ask for treatment in a period of time. As the exact number of patients is unknown beforehand we focus on empirical numbers of patients based on earlier periods and refer to expected numbers of patients in allocation process.

For a given allocation problem $a \in A_2$ a *random allocation* is defined by a probability distribution p on the set of feasible number pairs $F(a)$. For any problem $a \in A_2$ a random allocation rule g chooses a probability distribution $g(a) = p$ on $F(a)$. The set of random allocations is closed under finite lotteries on the probability distribution on $F(a)$.

We consider a lottery over feasible deterministic pairs of numbers of patients that can be treated under the given allocation problem. If P denotes the set of all probability distributions on $F(a)$ then for a given probability distribution $p \in P$ the probability that $x \in F(a)$ is chosen with $p(x)$. For a probability distribution p we denote the expected number of patients that can be treated in each group $t_i(p)$ as the number of treatments in group i. The expected number of treatments in each group is $t_i(p) = \sum_{x \in F} x_i p(x)$ for $i = 1,2$. A vector $t = (t_1(p), t_2(p))$ represents the expected number of patients that can be treated under the given allocation problem. Each t is generated by a probability distribution p on $F(a)$. All vectors t form a set T which is the convex hull of $F(a)$. T is the set of all vectors that represent expected number of treatments for each group under a given allocation problem.

Example 1

The following example shows a medical allocation situation $a = (q = 20; q_1 = 2; q_2 = 4; n_1 = 6; n_2 = 4)$. For example, we have dialysis patients in group 1 and patients with hemophilia A in group 2. Each patient in group 1 needs less quantity than a patient in group 2 who is more costly as she needs a special medication that stops bleeding after surgery.

Figure 4.1 shows the budget line q and feasible deterministic allocations of the given allocation problem a. The intersections of the grid determine standard treatment to a certain number of patients according to the given problem. Feasible allocations form a set $F(a)$. The following vectors of patients sets are feasible deterministic allocations under the allocation problem a: $(0,0)$, $(3,2)$, $(2,3)$, and $(4,3)$. There may be allocations that are feasible under the given

77

budget such as $(7,1)$ but due to that fact that only 6 patients in group 1 await treatment this allocation is not considered a feasible allocation under a. Among feasible deterministic allocations there are inefficient allocations. Clearly $(0,0)$ is an inefficient allocation in so far that more patients in both groups can be treated simultaneously. The allocation $(2,3)$ is a weakly Pareto optimal as the budget may yield treatment to two more patients in group 1 or one more patient in group 2. Finally, we have strongly Pareto efficient allocations such as $(4,3)$ which means that the budget is exhaustively allocated.

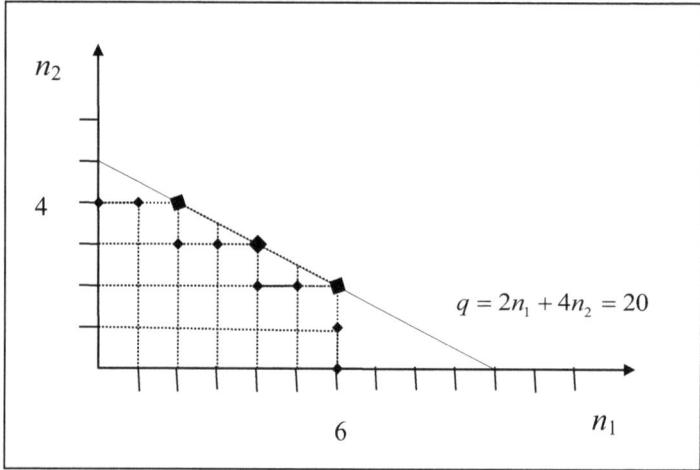

Figure 4.1: Feasible deterministic allocations for example 1 that are strongly and weakly Pareto efficient

Example 2 $a' = (q' = 20; q_1' = 2; q_2' = 4; n_1' = 10; n_2' = 4)$

From examples 1 through 3 we learn that the number of patients in a given allocation situation impacts the set of feasible alternatives. A typical medical allocation situation in this work may yield enough resources to each individual patients group, yet standard treatment to all is not feasible. We refer to example 1 if part of the budget suffices to treat each group individually. Then we may have a situation in which we may exhaustively allocate the total budget to either group which illustrates example 2, illustrated in figure 4.2.

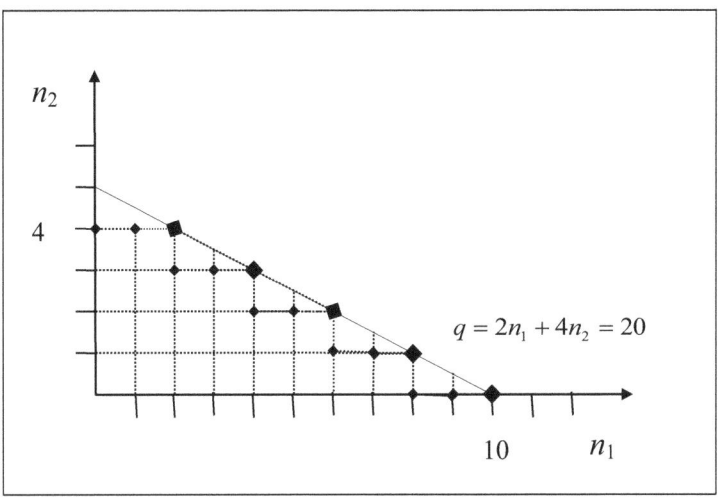

Figure 4.2: Feasible deterministic allocations for example 2 that are strongly and weakly Pareto efficient

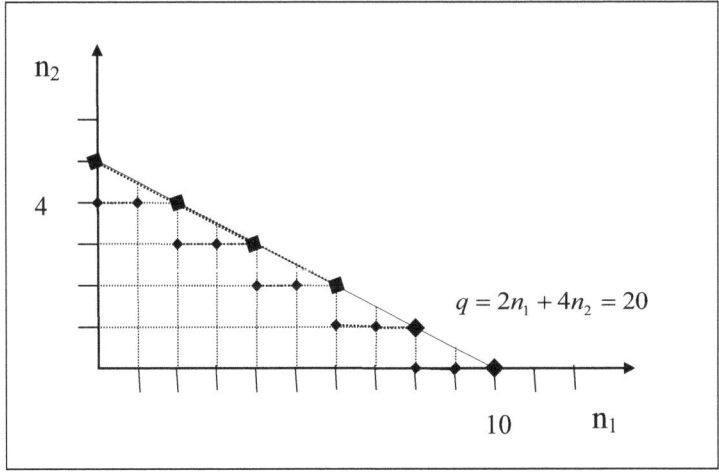

Figure 4.3: Feasible deterministic allocations for example 3 that are strongly and weakly Pareto efficient

Example 3 $\quad a'' = (q'' = 20; q_1'' = 2; q_2'' = 4; n_1'' = 10; n_2'' = 5)$

When the budget may be exhaustively spend to one or the other group, example 3 represents feasible deterministic allocations in figure 4.3.

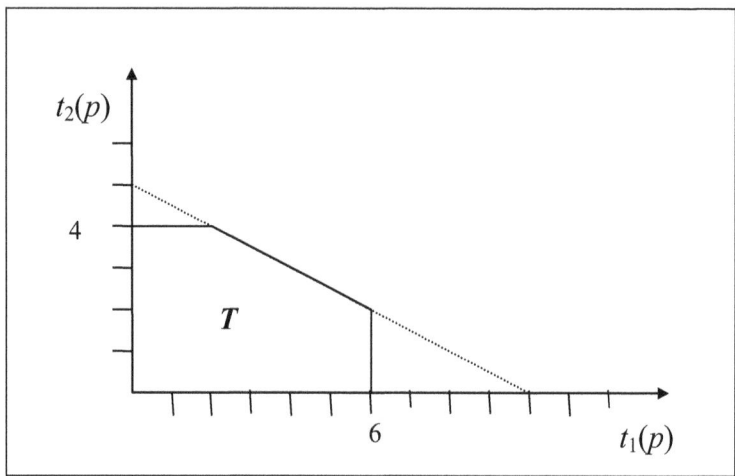

Figure 4.4: A set of expected number pairs of patients under example 1

A doctor may have an expectation how many people she may have to treat in a period of time. We express this expectation by a lottery over feasible deterministic allocations in figure 4.1.

These allocations form a convex hull of a treatment set T which is illustrated in figure 4.4. For example, if a random allocation mechanism chose vectors $(2,4)$ and $(6,2)$ with probability ½ and all other feasible deterministic allocations in $F(a)$ with zero probability, then a treatment vector $(4,3)$ represents expected numbers of patients who may receive standard treatment in each group. In addition to example 1 in figure 4.4, figure 4.5 illustrates the pairs of expected number of treatments (treatment sets) for example 2 and 3.

Studying different allocation problems that vary only in the number of patients that need treatment, we observe different shapes of sets of expected numbers of patients. In the model that we discuss here we allow the budget to cover at minimum the claims of one group, yet not all claims of all groups.

The treatment set is a pentagon shape as set T in figure 4.5, when part of the medical budget is enough to satisfy the claims of patients in either group. When the budget is enough to treat all patients in *one* group exhaustively then the shape of the set is a trapezoidal like set T' in figure 4.5. We arrive at a triangular shape when the budget is exhaustively sufficient to treat either group by itself. This refers to set T'' in figure 4.5.

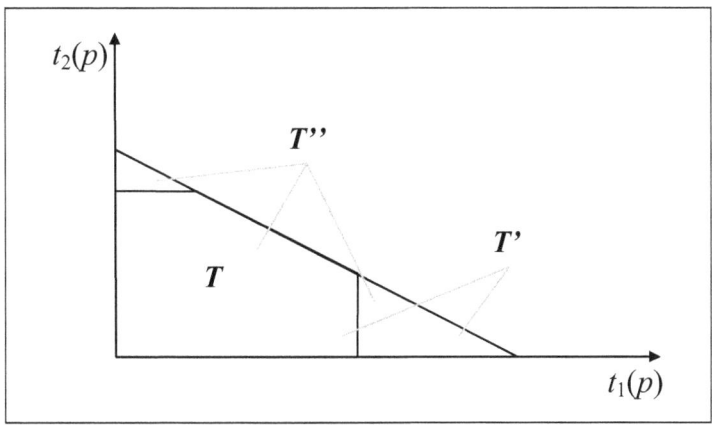

Figure 4.5: Different treatment sets

Summarizing this section, we used a similar approach to model a medical allocation situation. We modified two important aspects. First, we introduced two patients groups with a different number of patients that claim treatment. Second, we left success probabilities of the patients aside which means that the interpretation of this version of the model is different from chapter 3. While we discussed increases in success probabilities for each patients group, we focus on the number of standard treatments in each group.

4.3 A cooperative bargaining model

Next we use a cooperative bargaining approach to explain how the medical budget may be allocated to two groups of patients that each have an individual request based on guidelines of standard treatments. In the following we define notations from cooperative bargaining theory that we will use in the model.

We call the initial situation when no patient has yet been assigned treatment the *status quo* t^0 of a bargaining situation. Therefore, in this model the status quo is equivalent to the origin of the problem such that the vector $t^0 = (0,0)$ and we know that $t^0 \in T$.

If at least one group may increase the expected number of treated patients under the allocation mechanism we call this property strong *individual rationality* from the point of view of the group. For the allocation problem we assume that there exists an $t \in T$ such that $t > t^0$ (componentwise such that $t_i > 0$ for $i = 1,2$). If both groups may increase the expected number of treatments in the medical distribution process, we assume that they have an individual rational incentive to participate. For each patient it means that there is a positive chance of being treated under the given allocation problem compared to the status quo. The definition of the model meets the requirement of strong individual rationality and therefore excludes certain situations when the standard claim of a patient is too large to be covered either in one group or in both. This aspect then excludes the following three treatment sets $T = \{(0,0)\}$, $T = ch\{(0,0); (\overline{n_1}; 0)\}$ and $T = ch\{(0,0); (0, \overline{n_2})\}$.

An allocation situation with a defined status quo and feasible expected treatment alternatives is called a bargaining problem. A pair (T, t^0) with $T \in \widetilde{R}^{2+}$ and $t^0 \in T$ is called a *bargaining problem*, if there is at least one $t^0 \in T$ such that $t > t^0$ (componentwise $t_i > 0$ for $i = 1,2$). The domain of sets T is restricted to a two-dimensional space which we denote $\widetilde{R}^{2+}$ since $q, q_i, n_i \in \Re^+$. We use $\widetilde{B}^{2+}$ to denote the class of all two group bargaining problems (T, t^0) with all $T \in \widetilde{R}^{2+}$. Each bargaining problem is generated by an allocation problem a.

For each bargaining problem we look for a *bargaining solution* that describes an allocation of the resources. A function $f : \widetilde{B}^{2+} \to \widetilde{R}^{2+}$ such that for every $(T, t^0) \in \widetilde{B}^{2+}$ and $f(T, t^0) \in T$ holds is a solution on $\widetilde{B}^{2+}$. For a given allocation problem the solution to the bargaining problem is a consequence of a social agreement on desired properties. The corresponding allocation mechanism determines an expected number of patients that may receive standard treatment in each group. Typically the solution outcome allocates less treatment than needed to treat all patients. As the number of treatments translates into a division of the medical budget, scarce medical budgets then may not necessarily result in rejecting patients but in cutting patients' standard treatment. We further discuss this aspect as one of the results of this chapter in section 4.5.

4.4 Properties and solution concepts from cooperative bargaining theory

Since B^{2+} consists of different situations with status quo at the origin of the rectangle we have to model how the allocation should react on changes in the representation of the allocation problem. In detail, we allow a transformation from allocating numbers of treatment to allocating monetary units of a medical budget. We will assume that the groups do not make interpersonal comparisons. That means if e.g. the outcome number of treated patients in group 1 changes by some positive affine transformation into a problem of allocating units of the medical budget this should not affect the outcome in group 2 and vice versa. This implies that only the allocation to group 1 is changed according to her transformation.

Allowing positive affine transformations, we refer to a more general version of this axiom from cooperative bargaining theory. This type of transformation is a stronger condition and therefore a subset of the well-known transformations of invariance under positive affine transformation. The property describes a transformation from sets of expected-treatment-pairs to sets of medical-unit-pairs or medical-cost-pairs. This transformation requires a parameter v_i for all groups i with $v_i > 0$ which we interpret as monetary value per needed medical unit of q_i. Then we calculate medical value of treatment per patient in group i by $v_i \cdot q_i$ with $i = 1,2$ and respectively the medical value of a group is $v_i \cdot q_i \cdot t_i$.

Axiom B.INV (Invariance of budget transformation): Given a bargaining problem $(T,0) \in \widetilde{B}^{2+}$ and budget parameter v_i and individual needs q_i with $i = 1,2$ let a bargaining problem of allocating medical treatment cost $(M,0)$ be defined by $M = \{m \in \widetilde{R}^{2+} | \exists t \in T \text{ such that } m_i = v_i \cdot q_i \cdot t_i \text{ for } i = 1,2\}$. Then $f_i(M,0) = m_i \cdot f_i(T,0)$ for $i = 1,2$.

As a result, the solution of expected numbers of treatments is independent of such budget transformation. This axiom implies that a situation of allocating monetary units is equivalent to the initial situation of allocating medical units to patients groups as illustrated in figure 4.6. If the solution to the initial problem is independent of such a transformation, then we may in the following discuss treatment allocation problem $(T,0)$ and the results also apply to $(M,0)$ and vice versa.

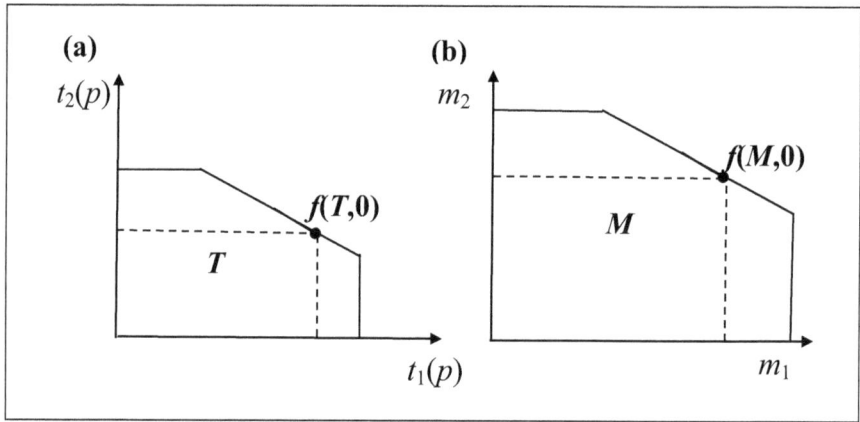

Figure 4.6: Changing the representation from allocating to patients (a) versus allocating budgetary units (b)

Axiom B.WPO (Weak Pareto optimality in allocating the budget): Given any $(T,0) \in B^{2+}$. If $t \in T$ and there exists another allocation $t' \in T$ such that $t' > t$ holds (componentwise: $t'_i > t_i$ for $i = 1,2$), then $t \neq f(T,0)$.

Weak Pareto optimality is desirable because it requires a solution to the bargaining problem such that bargaining cannot achieve a greater expected number of treatments for both groups simultaneously. It may be possible to treat more patients in one group with the other group remaining at the same number of treatments. WPO implies that a solution to the bargaining problem is vector of the weak Pareto optimal border of the treatment set.

Axiom B.SYM (Symmetry in budget allocation): Let $(T,0)$ be a symmetric bargaining problem in $\tilde{B}^{2+}$, i.e. for each $t \in T$ every permutation of t is also in T. Then $f_1(T,0) = f_2(T,0)$.

If we have a symmetric bargaining problem, we cannot distinguish between groups with respect to the requested quantity per patient and to the number of patients who need treatment in each group. Yet groups may differ in the type of illness, as this information is not included in the representation of the bargaining problem. The axiom requires that the solution to the problem is also symmetric.

Axiom B.IRR (Independence of irrelevant budget allocations): Suppose $(T,0)$ and $(T',0)$ are bargaining situation for allocation of number of treatments such that $T \subseteq T'$ and $f(T',0) \in T$. Then $f(T,0) = f(T',0)$.

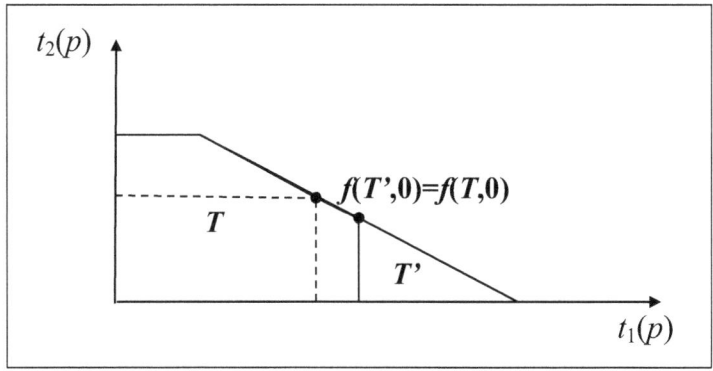

Figure 4.7: Independence of the bargaining solution of irrelevant treatment pairs

This property that is illustrated in Figure 4.7 implies that the number of patients in each group is of no concern to the allocation of the budget. Even in situations when justified claims of patients in one group are no longer considered the solution is to be divided by half. In extreme case that the request of one group falls short of half the budget, then that group is given the smaller requested amount and the entire rest is given to the other group.

For the class of bargaining problems in B^{2+} in cooperative bargaining theory, theorem 2.1 holds.

The Nash solution for two patients groups should be well defined since all axioms are well defined on the general class B^{2+}. Since we study here subsets of situation in B^{2+} all axioms should apply on a subclass $\widetilde{B}^{2+}$ as well.

Theorem 4.1: The Nash solution fulfils B.WPO, B.SYM, B.INV, and B.IRR on $\widetilde{B}^{2+}$.

Proof: The Nash solution is an allocation of medical resources that maximizes the geometric average of additional medial resources compared to the status quo. Since N is continuous and T is compact, the maximum Nash product $\max \Pi_{i=1,2}(t_i)$ is achieved at an allocation in T.

To see that N possesses B.WPO, imagine any solution vector that is not weakly Pareto optimal which is dominated by another solution that yields a better share of the resources to either patients group.

To see that N fulfils B.SYM, let (T,0) be a symmetric allocation problem with $\bar{t} = N(T,0)$. Let $\bar{\bar{t}}$ be any permutation of $\bar{t}$ such that $\bar{\bar{t}}_1 = \bar{t}_2$ and $\bar{\bar{t}}_2 = \bar{t}_1$. Then $\bar{t}$ and $\bar{\bar{t}}$ are allocations with equal average gains in medical allocations compared to the status quo. Since the maximum is achieved at a unique allocation in T, so $\bar{t} = \bar{\bar{t}}$ must hold. As $\bar{\bar{t}}$ was an arbitrary permutation it follows that $\bar{t}_1 = \bar{t}_2$.

To see that N fulfils B.INV, let ($\hat{M}$, 0) be a medical allocation problem derived from ($\hat{T}$,0) through a change of transformation parameter from medical unit into medical cost. An allocation vector m in M has coordinates $\hat{m}_i = v_i \cdot q_i \cdot \hat{t}_i$ for $i = 1,2$ and $\hat{t}$ is the corresponding allocation in $\hat{T}$. This transformation which is simply a constant multiplied to each allocation vector does not impact the solution allocation, so $f(\hat{M}, 0) = (v_i \cdot q_i)\, \mu_i(T,0)$ for $i=1,\ldots,n$.

To see that N fulfils B.IRR, imagine the Nash solution on a set and its subset. The solution allocation of the set is at least as large as on a subset. Thus the Nash solution on $\widetilde{B}^{2+}$ fulfils the four properties.

Examples

The following illustration shows the Nash solution for treatment sets T, T', and T'' which refer to allocation problems $a = (q = 20; q_1 = 2; q_2 = 4; n_1 = 6; n_2 = 4)$, $a' = (q' = 20; q_1' = 2; q_2' = 4; n_1' = 10; n_2' = 4)$ and $a'' = (q'' = 20; q_1'' = 2; q_2'' = 4; n_1'' = 10; n_2'' = 5)$.

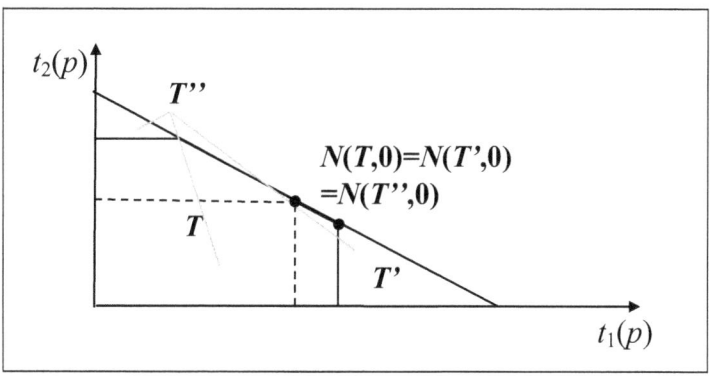

Figure 4.8: The Nash solution yields identical solutions for three treatment sets

Figure 4.8 shows that in both situations when compared to the triangle situation justified claims of each group are cut. Then in all three situations each group receives half the medical budget, which yields to cover standard needs of 5 patients in group 1 and 2.5 patients in group 2. The allocation of the medical budget is independent of justified claims of each group.

Figure 4.9 shows situations when compared to a triangular situation the claims of group 2 are cut dramatically such that the request of that group is smaller than half the budget. In this case group 2 receives the requested share of the budget and the rest is given to group 1.

After studying the Nash solution in detail we turn to the solution concept of Kalai/Smorodinsky.

For an analysis of the impact of increasing numbers of patients we refer to an axiom from cooperative bargaining theory which is individual monotonicity (Kalai/Smorodinsky (1975) and Kalai (1977)). It accounts for the idea that an existing group increases in size and all old group members give up part of their initial claim in order to accommodate other new members. Since we examine patients and their legitimate claims, the situation is very similar to our medical allocation problem. First of all, in our medical allocation problem we find that all have the same legitimate claim if they are members of a statutory health system. In addition, we observe the same need to sacrifice as the medical budget does not suffice to fulfill all claims completely. So, we call this discussed axiom monotonicity in numbers of patients and discuss how the solution of a medical bargaining situation under a given budget changes when new patients ask treatment in one group.

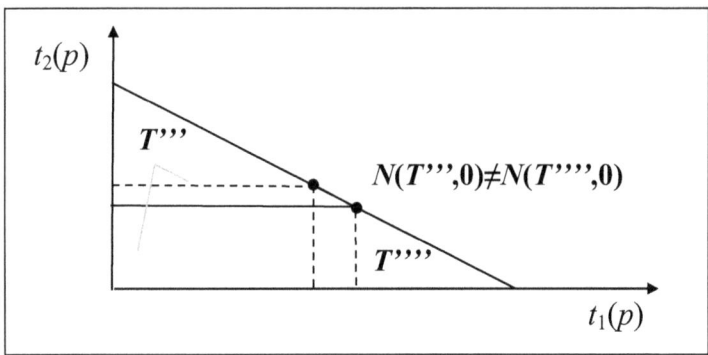

Figure 4.9: Two problems when the Nash concept yields different solutions

Next, we transfer the definition of individual monotonicity into a medical allocation situation. Imagine we have two medical bargaining situations $(T,0)$ and $(T',0)$ in two-dimensional space B^{2+} which refer to the following medical allocation situations a in hospital that reflects two succeeded periods :

$a = (q = 20; q_1 = 2; q_2 = 4; n_1 = 6; n_2 = 4)$

$a' = (q = 20; q_1 = 2; q_2 = 4; n_1' = 10; n_2 = 4)$.

Both situations differ only in the number of patients n_j in one group and equal in medical budget q as well as in individual group claims q_i. Therefore, conditions picture the case of two succeeding periods that differ only in the number of patients in one group, as illustrated in figure 4.10.

Axiom P.MON (Monotonicity in number of patients): Let $(T,0)$ and $(T',0)$ be two medical bargaining situations in $\widetilde{B}^{2+}$ with $n_j = n_j{'}$ for one j such that $T \subseteq T'$, then $f_i(T,0) \geq f_i(T',0)$ for $i \neq j$ with i,j =1,2.

The axiom requires that in a medical allocation situation when more patients require treatment under a scarce budget and otherwise same conditions patients of the original situation receive reductions in their treatment in order to accommodate new patients.

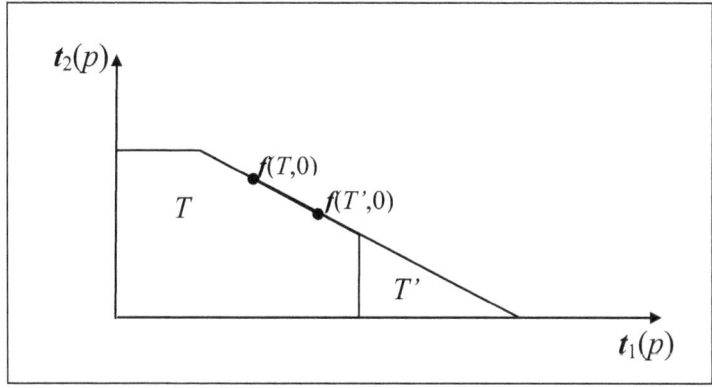

Figure 4.10: Patient monotonicity for two bargaining problems T and T'

According to the axiom, figure 4.10 shows that in a solution $f(T',0)$ not only the group, that increases, carries the burden of additional patients. As a fact, patients in group 2 in the final situation $(T',0)$ receive less compared to situation $(T,0)$. Group 1 receives the same reduction per patient in the initial situation, yet receives additional treatment for a new patient. As a result, when the number of patients in one group increases, reductions for both groups result. So far we did not discuss how resources are allocated within one group. In the section about results we discuss consequences of reducing treatment in each group.

Theorem 2.2 states that the Kalai/Smorodinsky solution is the only solution to satisfy weak Pareto optimality, scale invariance, symmetry, and restricted monotonicity in B^{2+}.

The Kalai/Smorodinsky solution for two patients groups should be well defined as well since all axioms are well defined on general class B^{2+} then. Since we study here subsets of situation in B^{2+} all axioms should apply on its subclass $\widetilde{B}^{2+}$ as well.

Theorem 4.2: The Kalai/Smorodinsky solution is a solution that satisfies B.WPO, B.SYM, B.INV, and P.MON on $\widetilde{B}^{2+}$.

Proof: The Kalai/Smorodinsky solution in theorem 4.2 is a well defined concept. There is an allocation t^* that minimizes the reductions in allocated medical units compared to patients' claims. Geometrically, the solution is an allocation on the line connecting status quo and ideal point. The Kalai/Smorodinsky solution is the maximal point $\mu(T,0)$ in T that fulfils $t^*_1/t_1 = t^*_2/t_2$. This leads to an equal relative reduction in medical claims compared to standard treatment $\overline{T}$.

Clearly μ possesses B.WPO, B.SYM, and B.INV, the proof is the same as in the Nash solution above.

To see that μ fulfils P.MON, imagine two allocation sets with identical status quo that are subsets and a line running from status quo to ideal point. Then a solution on the larger set is at least as large as on the subset.

Thus the Kalai/Smorodinsky solution fulfils all four axioms on $\widetilde{B}^{2+}$.

Example

In the following example we refer to the allocation problems:
$a = (q = 20; q_1 = 2; q_2 = 4; n_1 = 6; n_2 = 4)$ and

$a' = (q' = 20; q_1' = 2; q_2' = 4; n_1' = 10; n_2' = 4)$ that are illustrated for the Kalai/Smorodinsky solution in figure 4.11. The situations are different in so far that in a' four more patients ask treatment.

The solution under the Kalai/Smorodinsky concept shares medical resources such that group 1 receives approx. 8.6 units and group 2 receives 11.4 units. If we consider all 10 patients, a predetermined standard treatment cannot be given to all patients. (Under standard treatment 2.9 patients in group 1 and 4.3 patients in group 2 could be cured.) Instead, we assume that each patient receives less treatment than prescribed by guidelines. In a specific situation a doctor may approve of dismissing patients earlier from hospital than under standard therapy.

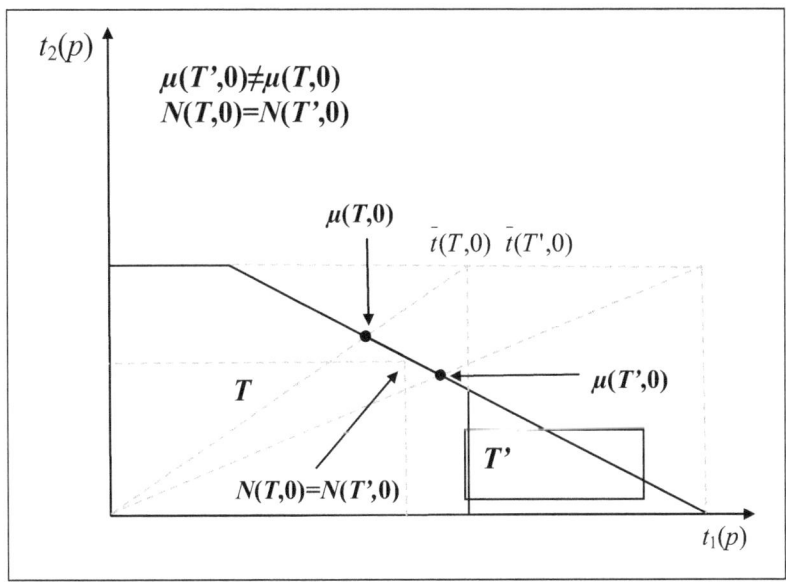

Figure 4.11: Kalai/Smorodinsky solution and Nash solution

In situation a' the budget is split such that 11.1 units to group 1 and 8.9 units to group 2. Again, standard treatment cannot be given to all patients. Compared to the original situation patients in group two receive less treatment although there are no additional patients in group 2. From figure 4.11 it is clear that these patients carry the burden of additional patients in group 1. Despite the new patients in group 1 all other patients also receive less treatment compared to the original situation. This fact cannot easily be seen in figure 4.11 since new and old patients are mixed in group 1. In the original situation patients claims toward treatment are reduced due to scarcity. When scarcity increases by additional patients, then all old patients have to reduce their claims accordingly such that all patients (including new patients) realize an identical proportional treatment compared to their standard treatment.

Compared to the Kalai/Smorodinsky solution, the Nash solution yields the same result for both allocation problems. This result is different from the solution of the Kalai/Smorodinsky solution. For our initial example in figure 2 the Nash solutions $N(T,0)$ and $N(T',0)$ yield half the medical resources to each group. Independent of the changes in the size of the group, the budget is shared by half under this concept. As a fact, in group 1 all original patients in T' receive less treatment than in T, which implies that they accommodate treatment to new patients in their group. On the other side, in group 2 all patients receive the same treatment in both situations. Treatment standards under the Nash solution change only for the group that increases.

Even though the concept of Kalai/Smorodinsky reflects an important quality of a health insurance system, the concept is limited in its application, since it is not well defined for the case of more than two groups (Roth 1979). Imai (1983) shows how the concept translates into problems with n>2. The author implies a weaker axiom of the IIA and RM to achieve a unique solution- the lexicographic maximin solution.

4.5 Results and conclusion

We applied cooperative bargaining theory to the simple case of two patients groups with different group size. The bargaining sets are triangles and quadrangles and pentagons that are created by different numbers of patients in each allocation problem. Here, the bargaining concepts of Nash and Kalai/Smorodinsky lead to different solutions. For two groups the Nash solution assigns equal proportional allocations, which means in the case of two groups each group receives half of the medical budget, as long as sharing half-half is a feasible solution. If not, the group that requests less than half the resources receives this amount and the rest is given to the other group. The Nash solution concept, as it is applied here, discriminates large groups and patients with large medical claims. In consequence this concept means that patients of different groups carry a different burden from scarcity of medical resources. The other concept we studied is the Kalai/Smorodinsky solution which allocates resources on the basis of group size and their claims. Under this allocation mechanism, each patient carries the same proportional burden due to scarce medical resources. This result makes the Kalai/Smorodinsky solution an interesting concept in the context of this model. The downside of this concept is that from bargaining theory we know it is problematic to extend the solution concept to more than two groups.

On the set of these special two-person cases the above Nash solution can be characterized by the properties of weak Pareto efficiency (B.WPO), symmetry (B.SYM), invariance under positive affine transformations (B.INV), and independence of irrelevant alternatives (B.IRR). According to weak Pareto efficiency, the number of treatments cannot be increased for both groups simultaneously under the given medical budget. The property of symmetry requires that the names of the patients and their respective illnesses do not matter. Allocation situations that have patients groups with identical group size and claims the distribution process leads to identical allocations of expected number of treatments. Transformation invariance refers to applicable positive affine transformations of the number of treatments. The solution of expected numbers of treatments is independent of such positive affine transformations. The fourth axiom of independence of irrelevant alternatives refers to a situation when justified claims of patients are no longer considered. According to the axiom, the Nash solution then does not change as long as the outcome to share equally is efficient.

An axiom that accounts for such an effect is monotonicity which we will call monotonicity in number of patients. When a new patient requires treatment then all patients in all groups carry the burden of the additional patient equally. Combined with the first three axioms of the Nash solution patient monotonicity characterizes the Kalai/Smorodinsky solution.

In the following we discuss different interpretations of the solutions under the two cooperative bargaining concepts. In detail, we follow two lines- either a chance or a budget allocation interpretation.

Under a chance allocation interpretation to receive standard treatment expresses just as in the first version of the model, that under the given allocation problem not all patients may receive standard treatment. According to the solution allocation standard treatment can be given to a certain a percentage of the group, which means that some patients may receive or may not receive treatment.

Another interpretation is the expected number of standard treatments in each group, which leads to the same conclusion, which is that some patients cannot receive treatment. In real allocation situation when the medical good is not divisible, such as in organ transplantation, this is a bitter reality. In this case we have e.g. waiting lists that use criteria such as compatibility, waiting time etc. Yet in this case, when the medical good may be split up in smallest increments, the solution may not necessarily mean to refuse treatment to patients.

Instead we may interpret the result as a reduction in standard treatment to all patients. Under a restricted medical budget, when not all medical claims of all patients may be fulfilled, then reducing standard treatment is a way to give some treatment to all patients. In fact this interpretation means that no patient can expect to receive standard treatment. If no patient can be treated according to medical standards, what goods seems medical progress in examinations and medications?

Both interpretations seem controversial at first glance. While the first is an all-or-nothing-decision, the second is a proportional reduction of medical treatment that leaves some space for additional measures in a statutory health system. The consequences of the reduction to each patient can be different for each medical allocation situation. In hospitals reducing standard treatment may mean to cut treatment time per patient. For doctors this means to reduce the time to visit, examine and treat patients as well as for nurses this means to reduce the amount of nursing time, even to reduce cleaning time. This example enables proportional reduction of standard treatment, as times per patient can be reduced proportionally. But how much can they be reduced? This question induces a discussion about minimal treatment standards for patients in the hospital. Additionally needed services may require co-payments and private insurance that pays for special doctor visits, single bedrooms and special nursing time. Again, the question comes up, how far can we reduce statutory services to patients that cannot afford private insurance. If reducing treatment time is considered, maybe we have to discuss a substitution of services. For example, reducing treatment time per visit with a doctor, while allowing nurses to take care of some specialized treatments in the laboratory, take blood pressure and blood samples, help with bookkeeping, organize an efficient allocation of appointments etc. Other medical area one of the following methods may be applied. Postponing of medical services surgery etc, as well as longer waiting time for doctor's appointment are popular methods for pushing cost to the next period when medical supply is scarce. Medication and medical services may be excluded from the treatment catalogue in case there cannot be proven a significant additional benefit to the patient. In general co-payments are regarded popular in terms of self-determination of patients.

Examining the Nash solution, we find that of all the above axioms monotonicity is not a property of that solution concept, because the axiom of independence of irrelevant alternatives is contradicting any monotonicity axiom (Kalai (1979)). Since we analyze subsets of bargaining set discussed in cooperative bargaining theory we find that patient monotonicity is not a property of the Nash concept either. The Nash solution in the two-group-case yields to each group the smaller of half the medical budget or the amount needed to treat all patients.

In contrast to the Nash solution concept assigns medical resources independent of group size and individual needs, the Kalai/Smorodinsky solution fulfils patient monotonicity. When medical supplies are scarce, under this concept each patient receives an equal proportional reduction in treatment compared to the initial claim. When a new patient claims treatment, the new solution also reflects this aspect. Consequently, the reduction in treatment for the old patients must be much greater than before in order to give comparative treatment to a new patient. The Kalai/Smorodinsky solution concept is sensitive to changes in the number of patients. Even though the number of patients changes only in group 1, all patients of all groups have to sacrifice their claims in equal portions for new patients. As a result, in the given medical allocation situation treatment standards under the Kalai/Smorodinsky concept are equally reduced for all patients when new patients ask treatment. The extent of treatment dramatically responds to the number of patients that ask treatment. As we discussed in an earlier, a reduction of treatment standards results for example in longer waiting time for doctor's appointments and medical examinations as well as shorter length of stay in hospitals (Younis/Forgione (2009)).

A further step may be the extension to more than two groups of patients. The property of strong Pareto efficiency is problematic for the concept of Kalai/Smorodinsky with more than two groups (Imai (1983)). We may apply a lexicographic solution concept such that we consider the needs of all groups according to some egalitarian principle which we still we have to derive. In addition we may be able to fulfill needs of patients in other groups.

In conclusion, we present a model which is able to deal with some specific types of medical allocation problems. If we generalize the problem to the case of two groups with different numbers of homogeneous patients, the classical bargaining solutions concepts of Nash and Kalai/Smorodinsky lead to different outcomes. We derive allocation mechanisms and their properties from normative cooperative bargaining theory. For the simple case of two patients, the proposed allocation mechanisms represent different egalitarian principles. While the Nash concept assigns equal shares of the budget to each group, the Kalai-Smorodinsky concept assigns equal relative burden to each patient compared to ideal treatment.

Further research with respect to two-group models will be to study different degrees of scarcity and the situation that the budget may be large enough to give patients more than their minimal needs. This was conducted in an experimental study by Ahlert et al. (2008). Another alternative of the model is the application of discrete bargaining theory, when bargaining sets are discrete. After analyzing two-group models, a further step may be the extension to more than two groups of patients. The generalization of the Nash solution will probably be straight forward. However, the property of strong Pareto efficiency is problematic for the concept of Kalai/Smorodinsky with more than two groups as it is with more than two persons (Roth (1979)). We will probably have to apply a lexicographic solution concept (c.f. Imai (1983)). This implies that first the needs of all patients in all groups are satisfied according to some egalitarian principle that still needs to be derived. Afterwards the expected health states of some patients can be increased further on in order to achieve Pareto optimality.

5 Different types of monotonicity in a cooperative bargaining model of distributing medical resources

5.1 Introduction

Allocating medical budgets among hospital departments can be tough, especially, when the budget is sufficient to give full treatment to each individual group yet not to all. For example, we have a medical allocation situation in which two patients groups compete over medical resources based on individual claims. Both groups differ in the type of disease, number of patients and medical quantity claimed. Patients in one group are identical with respect to type of disease and medical quantity needed to treat. In more detail, a large group of surgery patients without any other disorder stands face to face with a small group of hemophilia patients who need special medical treatment under surgery which is extremely expensive. So a large group of patients with small individual medical claim and a small group with an extremely high individual claim compete for scarce medical resources. Imagine that in preliminary bargaining process an agreement on what share of the budget each group receives has been achieved. Since the budget is restricted not all patients may be treated fully according to their claims. In fact, we allow partial treatment, that may relate discussed measures in chapter 4 such as postponing surgeries. In addition, we now examine how changes in the initial conditions affect the solution. Compared to the initial situation either the number of patients that claim treatment or patients' individual claims or the amount of medical resources available has changed. In our example of surgery patients, we may experience e.g., that more hemophilia patients need treatment than last period and therefore study how small changes in the beginning conditions impact allocation of resources and hence influence standard treatment. Analyzing this impact and distinguishing different types of monotonicity is the heart of this chapter.

The model in this paper refers to a medical allocation problem that has been discussed by Ahlert (2009) in a health economics context. It defines an allocation problem with a finite number of patients who each have an individual claim. The total amount of the medical good does not suffice to fulfill all needs. This paper considers this type of model and defines and analyzes solutions to such allocation situations. We apply cooperative bargaining theory and characterize allocation mechanisms by their normative properties. Finding solutions to the described allocation problem one may consider different solution concepts. Ahlert (2006) and Ahlert (2009) define a random solution mechanism for such an allocation problem. A second approach considers allocating medical resources according to a priority list as proposed by Ahlert (2005) and Zimmermann (2009). In addition to theoretical concepts, Ahlert et al. (2009) discuss their experimental work in medical allocation situations.

Finally, we continue the discussion in of chapters 3 and 4. In contrast to the two previous chapters, here we do not present another model. In continuation of chapter 4 we apply more normative axioms from cooperative bargaining theory. In particular, we focus on the bargaining concepts of Nash (1950) and Kalai/Smorodinsky (1975) that yield different solutions that we discuss in further detail. Thomson (1983) and Thomson/Lensberg (1989) discuss monotonicity axioms in a cooperative bargaining model which we will use in particular to define and analyze monotonicity axioms in a medical allocation situation.

In the following we will discuss three different properties of monotonicity that are derived from cooperative bargaining – monotonicity in patients (groups) in section 5.2 and 5.3, monotonicity in budgets (5.4), and monotonicity in needs (5.5). We motivate their use in a medical context, give definitions and application examples. In the end of each section we study these axioms under two different allocation mechanisms and discuss their application in a medical framework. Section 5.6. summarizes important results.

5.2 Monotonicity in patients groups

Before introducing more monotonicity axioms from cooperative bargaining theory, we give a more detailed insight into some aspects of the model. First, we explain how the property of monotonicity fits into the model and give examples. Second, we emphasize the role of patients' claims towards standard treatment. Last, we summarize results from the presented property of monotonicity in number of patients from chapter 4 and give some new implications for a statutory health system.

Strict Monotonicity as a property of a medical allocation process describes whether the allocated medical share either increases or decreases when the amount of resource or any other parameter of the initial situation steadily changes. For example, if the budget steadily increases, then, as a result, the allocation to each patient ought to increase and never decrease. The discussed monotonicity axioms are socially desired properties as they show how changes of initial conditions impact the final allocation outcome. We examine how these properties can be implemented in a medical allocation situation. Further, we discuss two allocation mechanisms that may or may not fulfill the property of monotonicity. For example, if we observe a decrease of a medical budget in a hospital by 20 % compared to last period and but the same number of patients to treat with identical claims, cutting claims is inevitable. The question is how the allocation mechanisms reduces patients' claims and whether each patient is treated equally with respect to the reduction of their claims.

In this chapter we study in what manner patients claims change in the new situation compared to the initial situation. Are patients' fulfilled claims of an earlier period to be reconsidered? If so, how do allocation mechanisms deal with enforceable rights? A medical need which is either manifested by heritage or by law and which can be confirmed by social or legal institutions is called an enforceable need or claim. We will use claim rather than need, since we put emphasis on the patients' entitlement to services from statutory health insurance as e.g. in Germany. In the last consequence these medical claims are derived from treatment standards which are treatment guidelines for patients as recommended by a doctor.

Medical enforceable claims are health services that patients are entitled to by law or heritage. In the German statutory health system each member's general entitlements to health services are written down in § 70 SGB V. Patients may claim medical treatment from paragraph 1 which states that medical suppliers ought to treat all patients equally and according to patients' needs and general medical standards. The Nikolaus decision from Dec. 6th 2005 (Az.1BvR 347/98), enforces medical claims of members in the German statutory health system for medical treatment in case of deadly diseases without standard therapy that have a minimal chance of improving the health status. If additional and often costly services are to be given to the patients we also have to care about the trade-off. Under a given medical budget the consequence is that other medical services are reduced or withdrawn from a treatment catalogue.

In addition to medical claims that are entitlements by law, the definition also includes a social aspect of claims by heritage. For instance, medical claims that patients realized of over many years ought to be reconsidered as well. For a long time the German statutory health system provided all-encompassing medical services to its members according to the latest medical research. With the dawn of many new medical examinations and technological inventions which lead to offering more and more medical services, the financial stability of the system is put on trial. Accordingly, we have to revise long-existing medical claims.

After putting emphasis on the definition of monotonicity and medical claims, we use some results of chapter 4 on monotonicity in patients that relate to the discussion in this chapter.

In medical allocation situations we may find examples in which an increasing or decreasing number of patients needs treatment compared to the last period under otherwise identical conditions.

Monotonicity in number of patients as discussed in chapter 4 comes from the well-known property of individual monotonicity from cooperative bargaining. We have translated the meaning into the medical context. As a result we find that we study changes in medical allocation situations in which the number of patients increases or decreases. For example, we have a situation in which more patients than expected need medical treatment, either caused by epidemic diseases or closing doctors' practices. Another reason may be the introduction of new screening methods and other new technological inventions that causes additional treatments such as mammography screening. In case of a positive diagnosis patients receive additional examinations such as biopsy. While discussing increasing number of patients, we may also discuss the opposite situation. When medical treatment becomes obsolete due to new technical inventions or medications, then fewer patients need treatment. For example, the immunization against children's diseases reduces the number of treatments for pocks, rubella and so on.

Findings from chapter 4 state that monotonicity in number of patients results in reductions in treatment standards among old patients in order to accommodate new patients. In medical situations with scarcity and legitimate treatment claims of all patients, original treatment standards cannot be sustained when more patients ask treatment.

On the one hand, the Nash solution does not fulfill the PMON. In medical situations with scarcity and legitimate treatment claims of all patients, the reduction in treatment standards under the Nash solution are carried unilaterally by that group that increases in size.

The Kalai/Smorodinsky solution, on the other hand, fulfills the axiom of patient monotonicity which means that in a given allocation problem all patients in all groups receive the same proportional reduction in treatment standards. Studying decreasing numbers of patients yields a greater share of the medical budget to each patients compared to a situation with a larger group of patients.

5.3 Monotonicity in number of patients groups

We cannot only think of situations in which more *patients* need treatment, but we may also have situations in which a new group of patients may claim treatment. To illustrate an example we simply extend the surgery case of appendix and hemophilia surgery patients by another group called cancer surgery patients. Research states that patients with liver cancer for example have higher chances to survive when they undergo special surgery in addition to chemical therapy. There is a new treatment method for these patients and this group asks their share of the medical budget in a hospital.

In cooperative bargaining theory an axiom published by Thomson/Lensberg (1989) is originally called population monotonicity. The axioms explains how a situation and the corresponding solution change when the number of agents changes. As a new agent comes in, this person has presumably the same legitimate claim as anyone else. Allocating a fraction to all agents means that the old agents need to sacrifice in order to give to the new agent. The idea of the axiom is to avoid a situation in which any of the old agents is better off. So all agents ought to share according to the responsibilities in the situation, which expresses some form of solidarity.

In analogy to the Thomson/Lensberg axiom we compare two situations – one with two and another with an additional patients group. Coming back to our surgery example of an additional group that asks treatment we study the following question. Assuming that budgetary restraints remain the same and all claims of all patients are legitimate, how are medical resources allocated when new treatment methods are available?

In analogy to population monotonicity we introduce an axiom that we call monotonicity in number of patients groups. We will apply the axiom in the context of a medical allocation problem. Drawing upon the surgery example we have a situation $(T^2,0)$ which involves two patients groups and a situation $(T^3,0)$ that involves three groups. Both situations refer to the following allocation problems which differ in the total number of patients due to an additional patients group:

$$a^2 = (q = 24; q_1 = 2; q_2 = 2; n_1 = 9; n_2 = 6;)$$
$$a^3 = (q = 24; q_1 = 2; q_2 = 2; q_3 = 4; n_1 = 9; n_2 = 6; n_3 = 6).$$

According to Thomson and Lensberg (1989) the enlarged problem in three-dimensional space R^{3+} can be projected onto the coordinate space R^{2+} so that we receive a problem $(T^{3'},0)$. Since we consider comprehensive sets, $T^{3'}$ is equivalent to T^2. In detail, the allocation share that patient group 1 receives in problem $(T^2,0)$ is equivalent to the shares in $(T^{3'},0)$ and $(T^3,0)$ respectively. The same is true for patient group 2. This implies that the projection of a solution of $(T^3,0)$ onto coordinate subspace of $(T^2,0)$ is weakly dominated by the solution outcome for $(T^3,0)$. The requirement that $T^{3'}$ coincides with T^2 implies that arrival of a new patients group is not followed by external effects. The situations illustrated in figure 5.1 and 5.2 are such that patients groups can compare what claim they realize in situation $(T^2,0)$, $(T^{3'},0)$ and $(T^3,0)$.

Axiom PGMON (Monotonicity in number of patients groups): Let $T^2 \in \widetilde{B}^{2+}$ and $T^3 \in \widetilde{B}^{3+}$, let $(T^2,0)$ be a bargaining situation in R^{2+} and $(T^3,0)$ in R^{3+} and $(T^{3'},0)$ is a projection of $(T^3,0)$ onto R^{2+}, if $(T^2,0) = (T^{3'},0)$ then $f(T^2,0) \geq f(T^{3'},0)$.

In the following two paragraphs we discuss how the property of monotonicity in number of patients groups may be implemented in a set of axioms that define an allocation rule.

The Nash solution does not fulfill the property of population monotonicity (Thomson (1983)). Its axiom of independence of irrelevant alternatives contradicts fulfilling a monotonicity axiom. Compared to cooperative bargaining we examine subsets of cooperative bargaining sets which leads us to assuming that the Nash solution in our medical allocation problem does not fulfill monotonicity in number of patients groups. In fact, the Nash concept in this medical allocation situation leads to sharing the budget equally among the groups unless one group can be fully treated with less. For our example this means that the budget is either shared by two or three groups regardless of group size. In consequence this means that patients of different groups suffer different reductions in their claims. When an additional group asks for treatment, claims of all other patients are reduced, yet not proportionally to their claims.

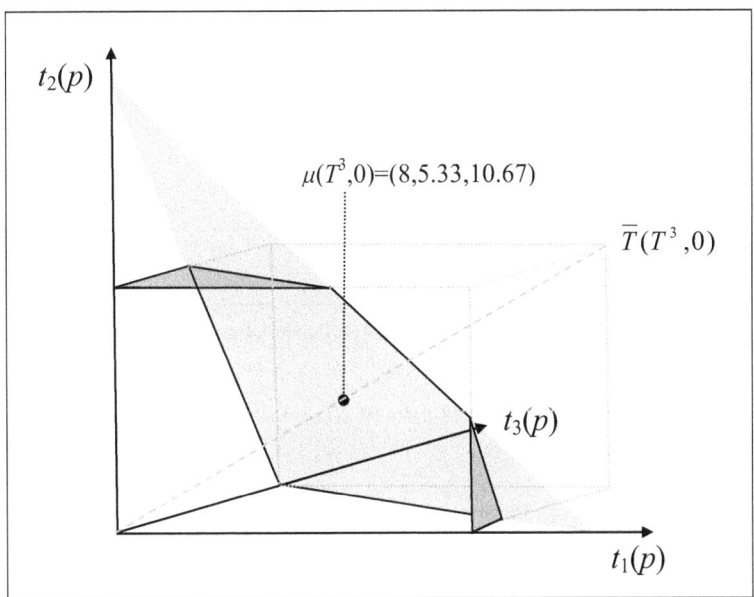

Figure 5.1: Kalai/Smorodinsky solution for three patients groups

Since the definition of the Kalai/Smorodinsky solution for $n > 2$ conflicts with Pareto optimality (Roth (1979)), Thomson/Lensberg (1989) define population monotonicity and proof that the Kalai/Smorodinsky solution holds for more than two groups under a stronger set of axioms .

In order to define the Kalai/Smorodinsky solution for the case of more than two patients groups we have to discuss one two properties. We have already defined the properties B.WPO, B.SINV, and P.MON for medical allocation situations, yet we will restate them in the appropriate n-dimensional version.

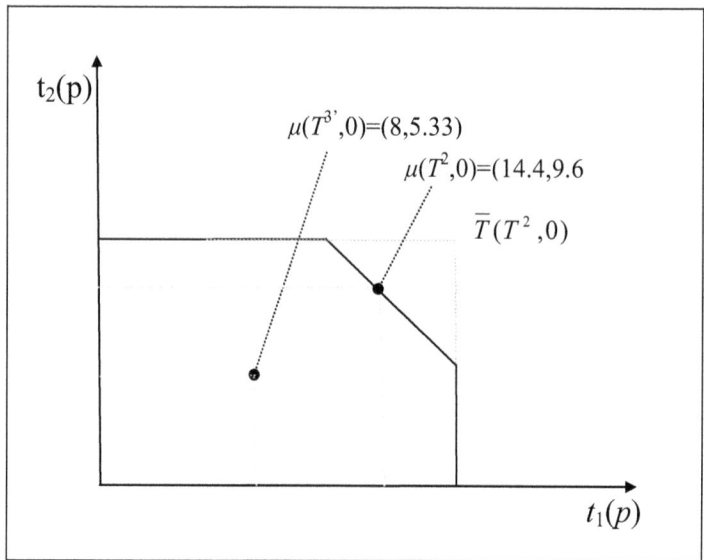

Figure 5.2: Projected Kalai/Smorodinsky solution for three patients groups

First, we present the n-dimensional form of weak Pareto optimality.

Axiom B.WPO' (Weak Pareto optimality of budget allocation): Given any $(T,0) \in \widetilde{B}^{n+}$. If $t \in T$ and there exists another allocation $t' \in T$ such that $t' > t$ holds (componentwise: $t'_i > t_i$ for $i = 1,...,n$), then $t \neq f(T,0)$.

The following axiom is a more general requirement of symmetry which we defined earlier.

Axiom B.AN (Anonymity in budget allocation): Let $\pi: \{1,...,n\} \to \pi: \{1,...,n\}$ be a permutation. Given $\tilde{t} \in R^n$, let $\tilde{\pi}(t): \{t_{\pi(1)},...,t_{\pi(n)}\}$ and $\tilde{\pi}(\tilde{t}) \equiv \{t' \in R^n \mid \exists t \in T \text{ with } t' = \tilde{\pi}(t)\}$. Then $f[\tilde{\pi}(T,0)] = \tilde{\pi}[f(T,0)]$.

Two societies of equal numbers of groups and group size and individual need will solve the allocation problem in the same way no matter what the characteristics of the patients (groups). Patients characteristics are names whereas patients groups characteristics are medical need and group size. The information required to come to a solution is based on the description of the medical bargaining problem. A permutation of characteristics of patients (groups) will lead to an identical permutation of the allocated medical amount.

The following axiom is explained earlier, so we simply present its n-dimensional representation.

Axiom B.INV' (Invariance of budget transformation): Given a bargaining problem $(T,0) \in \tilde{B}^{n+}$ and budget parameter v_i and individual needs q_i with $i = 1,...,n$ let a bargaining problem of allocating medical treatment cost $(M,0)$ be $M = \{m \in R^{n+} \mid \exists t \in T \text{ such that } m_i = v_i \cdot q_i \cdot t_i \text{ for } i = 1,...,n\}$. Then $f_i(M,0) = m_i \cdot f_i(T,0)$ for $i = 1,...,n$.

The following axiom represents situations with small differences.

Axiom B.CONT (Continuity in budget allocation): If $T^k \to T$ and $t_0^k \to t_0$ in the Hausdorff topology[28], then $f(T^k, t_0^k) \to f(T, t_0)$.

The property of continuity describes that small changes in the initial condition of the medical allocation problem lead to small changes in the allocation of medical resources. This property may become important when new patients need treatment or when a person's need increases a bit. Then all patients do not have to fear dramatic changes in their share of medical treatment.

Last, we present the *n*-dimensional version of population monotonicity.

---

28 The Hausdorff topology is a topological space in which any two distinct allocations are element in two different allocation sets that are disjoint.

Axiom PG.MON (Monotonicity in number of patients groups): Let $T^n \in \widetilde{B}^{n+1}$ and $T^{n+1} \in \widetilde{B}^{n+1}$, let $(T^n,0)$ be a bargaining situation in R_+^n and $(T^{n+1},0)$ in R_+^{n+1} and $(T^{(n+1)'},0)$ is a projection of $(T^{n+1},0)$ onto R_+^n, if $(T^n,0) = (T^{n+1},0)$ then $f(T^n,0) \geq f(T^{(n+1)'},0)$.

From cooperative bargaining we know that the following theorem holds.

The Kalai/Smorodinsky solution is the only solution to satisfy weak Pareto optimality, anonymity, scale invariance, continuity and population monotonicity in B^{n+} (compare theorem 2.3).

Since we study subsets of the situations in cooperative bargaining theory, some results apply to our work as well. The Kalai/Smorodinsky solution for more than two patients groups should be well defined as well since all axioms are well defined on general n-dimensional space B^{n+} then. As we study here subsets of situation in B^{n+} all axioms should be applicable on a smaller space as well and yield a solution in $\widetilde{B}^{n+}$.

Theorem 5.1: The Kalai/Smorodinsky solution is a solution that satisfies weak Pareto optimality, anonymity, invariance of budget transformation, continuity and monotonicity in number of patients groups in $\widetilde{B}^{n+}$.

Proof. The Kalai/Smorodinsky solution in theorem 5.1 is a well defined concept. It is easy to see that μ possesses B.WPO' and B.INV'.

To see that μ fulfils B.AN, let $(T,0)$ be an allocation problem with $t' = \mu(T,0)$. Let t'' be any permutation of t' such that $t'' = \pi(t') = (t'_{\pi(1)},...,t'_{\pi(n)})$. Then t' and t'' are allocations with equal average reductions in medical allocations compared to standard treatment $\overline{T}$. Since the maximum is achieved at a unique allocation in T, it must hold that $t'' = \mu(\pi(T,0))$.

To see that μ fulfils B.CONT, let t and t^k be to allocations in T whereby t^k is only marginally different from t e.g. there is one more patient in group 1. Then the solution ought not change by much.

To see that μ fulfils PG.MON, imagine two allocation problems with identical status quo that are subsets and another patients group in the second problem. Then a solution on the smaller problem is as least as big as in the larger problem.

Thus the Kalai/Smorodinsky solution fulfils all 5 axioms on $\tilde{B}^{n+}$.

The Kalai/Smorodinsky solution as defined under theorem 2 fulfills monotonicity in number of patients groups. When medical resources are scarce and new patients groups ask treatment each patient receives an equal proportional reduction in treatment compared to the initial claim. In contrast to the Nash solution this concept is sensible to the number of groups that ask treatment.

Example
Let us study an example in order to compare solutions under the Nash and the Kalai/Smorodinsky concept in two and three-group cases. We are given the following allocation situation:
$a = (q = 24; q_1 = 2; q_2 = 2; q_3 = 4; n_1 = 9; n_2 = 6; n_3 = 6)$.

The solutions for both situations in three and two-dimensional space are illustrated in figures 5.1 respectively 5.2. We see that the group 1 and group 2 receive less treatment in the larger group and their reduction helps to treat group 3. In more detail, the Nash solution for T^2 is $N(T^2,0) = (12,12)^{29}$ and for T^3 $N(T^3,0) = (8,8,8)$. In contrast, the Kalai/Smorodinsky solution yields $\mu(T^3,0) = (8, 5.33, 10.67)$ and for the initial situation $\mu(T^2,0) = (14.4, 9.6)$. In both concepts groups 1 and 2 receive a reduction in the allocated budget. While the Nash solution cuts budgets for the old group independent of group size or need, the Kalai/Smorodinsky solution accounted for these two criteria. In fact, all groups have to give up the same proportional share of their initial claims which in this case is 55,56% for $(T^3,0)$ and 20% for $(T^2,0)$. Keep in mind that the reduction under the three-group-case must be greater since another group has to be accommodated.

Summarizing both solution concepts we find that the Kalai/Smorodinsky solution represents an important property of a statutory health system. Monotonicity in number of patients groups under the Kalai/Smorodinsky concept assures two principles – solidarity among patients and equality of

---

29   The solution outcome in this paragraph is given in quantities of the medical budget and easily converted into number of full treatments by dividing by q_i.

burden. Solidarity among patients groups means that new groups can be accommodated and in addition it assures equality among old patients groups in so far that under the new treatment standard each group suffers the same proportional loss of medical budget compared to the initial situation.

In the end we shortly discuss situation with decreasing patients groups. A patients group may not ask treatment due to new research results. For example, a few years ago simple cold medicine such as nasal sprays were discarded from the list of covered services under the German statutory health system. As a result, members have to pay for these medicines out of their own pockets. Here, for our model this leads to more resources available for the remaining groups. So in this case we observe just the opposite results as in the case of an additional patients group. Monotonicity in patients groups demands that each group benefits from freed resources.

Concluding this section we summarize our results. First, we defined and analyzed an axiom from cooperative bargaining theory which we call monotonicity in number of patients groups. It demands that under the given allocation problem an additional group receives treatment such that all other patients group give up part of their claims. Second, the Nash solution does not fulfill this property. It does not account for number of groups and their claims. Third, the Kalai/Smorodinsky solution on the other hand does fulfill monotonicity in number of patients groups such that an additional group is accommodated by reducing the claims of all other by an equal proportional share. Last, we found that the reverse case of decreasing patients groups reveals opposite results such that remaining patients groups benefit from a less scarce medical budget.

5.4 Resource monotonicity

In the following section we turn to another type of monotonicity – budget monotonicity. We analyze the question how does the solution to a medical allocation problem change, when the medical budget shrinks or grows. To be more specific we discuss reasons why the budget shrinks or grows and give examples. Then we define and translate an axioms from cooperative bargaining theory and apply it to our medical allocation problem. Next, we discuss different solution.

In the beginning we discuss the reasons why medical budgets fluctuate. First of all we may observe changes in the number of insured persons due new memberships and ended memberships (either by death or change to private insurers etc). More or less patients insured may cause the budget to fluctuate. Furthermore, it is possible that contribution percentages change which also influences total contributions. Assuming that contribution percentages are constant and we look at per capita budgets, we may still observe fluctuations in the medical budget. Since contributions are a fraction of members' monthly income, it is not surprising that the medical budget depends on economic cycles. The better off the economy is the more members are employed and pay contributions up to a maximum premium and the more members are in unemployment the more pay the minimum premium. The question is how do fluctuations in the medical budget affect treatment standards for patients in a statutory health insurance system? Therefore, we discuss the situation of shrinking budgets in detail, because patients, doctors etc are much more affected and this situation forces to apply some allocation rule.

For our following analysis we assume that fluctuations in the budget are caused by external effects such as the business cycle. We analyze a situation with a constant number of insured members which allows to look at per capita increased budgets. In addition we assume a constant contribution rate, since we hardly observe decreasing rates which would cause a decreasing budget.

We may imagine a situation in the hospital that has to give treatment to a fix amount of patients and receives a share of the overall medical budget. Due to higher lay-off rates more members pay the minimum premium which leads to a 20 % decrease in medical budgets compared to last year. How are the two groups of surgery patients treated with fewer resources but identical legitimate claims as last year if deficits in the medical budget are not compensated by tax revenues?

Example

Before studying the theoretical background of budget monotonicity we look at an illustrative example of two groups, with varying budgets and otherwise identical conditions. For example in figure 5.3, we have a situation

$a = (q = q^*; q_1 = 2; q_2 = 4; n_1 = 6; n_2 = 4)$ and all situations differ in the amount of the available resource ($q^*=8,12,16,20,28$). Starting from $q=28$, when all needs in all groups could be satisfied, we notice that with decreasing budgets the budget line moves toward the origin and restricts feasible allocations.

all types of allocation situations from full treatment to no treatment.

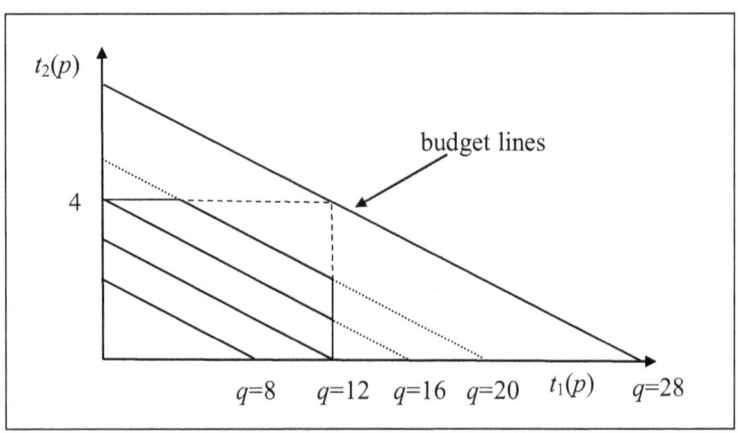

Figure 5.3: Different medical budgets

From figure 5.3 we also learn different degrees of scarcity. First, when the amount of the budget in our example is equal to or exceeds 28, we may have a situation in which both groups could be entirely treated. Second, we may have a situation in which both groups individually could be treated, yet not both entirely. In the example this is the case when $16 \le q < 28$. Third, scarcity increases when $12 \le q < 16$. Then only one group could be treated individually. Fourth, when the budget keeps on decreasing to $0 < q < 12$, then resources may be that scarce that not even one group could be entirely treated. Last, but not least we may theoretically have a situation in which no resources are available such that $q = 0$. This list describes

In this section we focus on medical scarcity situations in which resources typically yield to treat each group individually yet full treatment of all groups is not feasible. In the following we therefore, analyze the above mentioned second type of scarcity.

Studying these allocation situations through the eyes of cooperative bargaining we may apply the property of restricted monotonicity (Kalai/Smorodinsky (1975) and Roth (1979)). Given the maximum claims of each agent, restricted monotonicity demands that each agent in the enlarged situation ought to receive at least the same as in the initial situation. Restricted Monotonicity is a weaker property compared to individual monotonicity.

Applying this property to the context of a medical allocation problem, we use the notation budget monotonicity. In detail, we have two medical situations T and T' in the positive two-dimensional space B^{2+} that differ only in the amount of available resource such that T stems from a problem $a = (q; q_1; q_2; n_1; n_2)$ and T' from $a' = (q'; q_1; q_2; n_1; n_2)$ with $q' > q$.

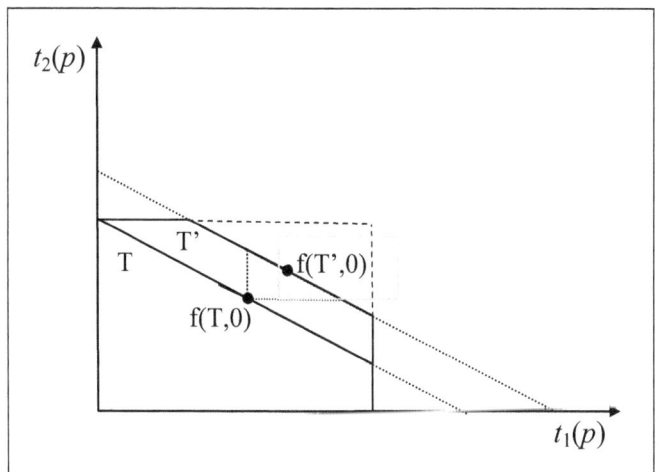

Figure 5.4: Budget monotonicity

Axiom B.MON (Budget Monotonicity): Let $(T,0)$ and $(T',0)$ be bargaining situations in B^{2+} and $T \subseteq T'$ then $f(T',0) \geq f(T,0)$.

The property of budget monotonicity demands that patients in a situation $(T,0)$ with a higher degree of scarcity as in do not receive better treatment compared to a situation $(T',0)$ with a lower degree of scarcity. Therefore the solution $f(T',0)$ depends on $f(T,0)$. As a result, treatment standards depend on the degree of scarcity caused by fluctuation of the budget (compare figure 5.4).

Next, we discuss if budget monotonicity can be a property of an allocation rule. Therefore, we study two concepts from cooperative bargaining - the Nash and the Kalai/Smorodinsky solutions.

We know that the Nash solution fulfills the axiom of irrelevant alternatives which makes this solution concept incompatible with a monotonicity property (Roth (1979)). This result applies to our allocation problems as well since they are subsets of situations in cooperative bargaining problems. The Nash solution applied to this medical allocation problem means that the each group receives either half the budget or its claimed share whatever is smaller. Sharing the budget this way does not account for the group and claim size. Fewer medical resources to share means that each patients groups' share reduce by the same amount, no matter how many patients in each group and no matter what they claim.

In contrast, the Kalai/Smorodinsky solution fulfills restricted monotonicity in the two-group case (Kalai (1975), Roth (1979)).

The Kalai/Smorodinsky solution is the only solution to satisfy invariance under positive affine transformations, weak Pareto optimality, symmetry, and restricted monotonicity in B^2 (compare theorem 2.2).

Since we showed that restricted monotonicity as well as all other axioms of the Kalai/Smorodinsky solution can be applied in this medical allocation problem Köckeritz (2009) we may apply this solution concept. As we study subsets of alternative sets in cooperative bargaining literature we assume that results apply here as well.

Theorem 5.2: The Kalai/Smorodinsky solution satisfies invariance under positive affine transformations, weak Pareto optimality, symmetry, and budget monotonicity in $\widetilde{B}^{2+}$.

Proof: The Kalai/Smorodinsky solution in theorem 5.2 is a well defined concept.

Clearly μ possesses B.WPO, B.SYM, and B.INV, the proof is the same as in the proof to theorem 5.1 above.

To see that μ fulfils P.MON, imagine two allocation sets with identical status quo that are subsets and a line running from status quo to ideal point.

Then a solution on the larger set is at least as large as on the subset. Thus the Kalai/Smorodinsky solution fulfils all four axioms on $\widetilde{B}^{2+}$.

Budget monotonicity under the Kalai/Smorodinsky solution demands that a medical budget is shared according to the claims of each patients group. When resources become even more scarce then each group's claims are reduced proportional. This solution concept is sensible to the number of patients that ask treatment.

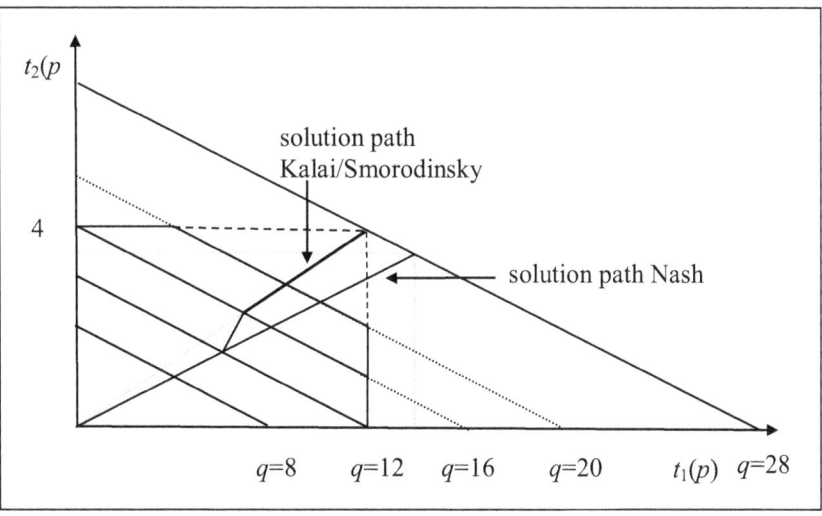

Figure 5.5: Solution paths for the Kalai/Smorodinsky and the Nash concept

Next, we study a solution path for both solution concepts independent of the axiom of budget monotonicity in order to compare both concepts. Figure 5.5 illustrates solutions for both concepts in allocation situations with varying medical resources. We notice that in situations with high degrees of scarcity, that is the budget does not suffice to treat even one group entirely, both concepts yield the same solution. When at least one group could be entirely treated then both concepts yield different solutions. According to Nash the budget is split by half independent of number of patients whereas the Kalai/Smorodinsky solution shares proportional depending on the number of patients. The latter case contains the type of scarcity that we study in this work. For all allocation problems studied in this work both concepts yield different solutions.

Concluding the analysis of solution concepts and budget monotonicity we discuss the importance of budget monotonicity in a statutory health system. From the definition of budget monotonicity we learn that the coverage of medical treatment of patients under a statutory health system ought to depend on the available budget which fluctuates due to economic changes. Keeping in mind the financial stability of this public sector treatment standards ought to be at least to some degree flexible to keep in the balance. Facing a situation in which treatment standards must be reduced due to shrunk budget, the decision is whether to cut the budget in even pieces and allocate to each group independent of group and claim size or to share the budget according to these to criteria. This in fact, is what the Kalai/Smorodinsky solution proposes and seem less arbitrary than the allocation under the Nash concept.

Before concluding this paragraph, we shortly discuss the case of increasing budgets. The reason why the budget may grow per capita may be due to increased contribution rates or economic growth. In medical allocation situation when we have more resources to allocate compared to last period we may also apply the solution concepts studied above. In the end, we find that the above results apply just analogously. Therefore, budget monotonicity demands that no patient receives less in the less scarce situation compared to a more scarce situation.

Summarizing the results in this section we first find that budget monotonicity in a medical allocation problem under scarcity leads to reductions in treatment standards. Second, while the Nash solution assigns half the budget or if less the asked claim, the Kalai/Smorodinsky solution accounts for group and claim size. Third, for the degree of scarcity studied here both concepts lead to different solutions. Last, in case of decreasing budgets resources become more scarce and hence patients ought to be not better of in the more scarce situation. Results apply for the case of increasing budgets in the same way.

5.5 Monotonicity in claims

In this section we discuss how a change in claims of patients impacts the allocation of scarce medical resources. We analyze what causes a change in claims, define an property of monotonicity in claims and explain how this may be a property of an allocation rule and how it may affect treatment standards. Medical claims of patients are indicated by a physician who follows medical guidelines. The discussion of claims in this cooperative bargaining model is separate from the theory of cooperative bargaining over claims as proposed by Bossert (1992) and Chun/Thomson (1992).

One reason why claims of patients may increase is due to increased prices for medical goods. An increase in prices for medical goods may be caused by increased production and transportation for pharmaceuticals. This is not a very strong argument as medical goods tend to become less expensive over time when patents protections run out. Moreover, with the availability of medication in online-pharmacy prices for medications are in general 30% lower than over the counter.

More likely, increases in prices result from investments in new medical technology. New medical goods may be more expensive due to financial investments compared to established medical treatment methods. Yet new technology may be more efficient, a less invasive therapy for patients. Old technology on the other hand may still enable sufficient treatment and generally uses less resources. When new treatment methods or medications become available this generally results in higher costs which leads to higher claims.

For example, there are new x-ray machines for the better detection of breast cancer. The therapy is costly, yet helps to detect early stages of breast cancer and may be a recommended treatment for some women. This new available technology leads to a change in recommended treatment standard at least for some patients which causes higher overall medical cost. As a results, we expect that increased claims of patients lead to greater shortage in medical resources.

Example

In the following example we built upon two medical allocation problems: $a = (q = 20; q_1 = 2; q_2 = 4; n_1 = 6; n_2 = 4)$ and

$a' = (q = 20; q_1' = 4; q_2 = 4; n_1 = 6; n_2 = 4)$.

We imagine it is the known surgery example. For patients in group 1 we have a new treatment method for example keyhole surgery available. The application of this new less invasive surgery method is more expensive since new medical technology need to be employed. Let us assume that the new technology is only to the benefit of patients in group 1 and therefore ought to be given to them exclusively. Compared to initial treatment, patients in group 1 use up twice as much per treatment. Figure 5.6 illustrates this example.

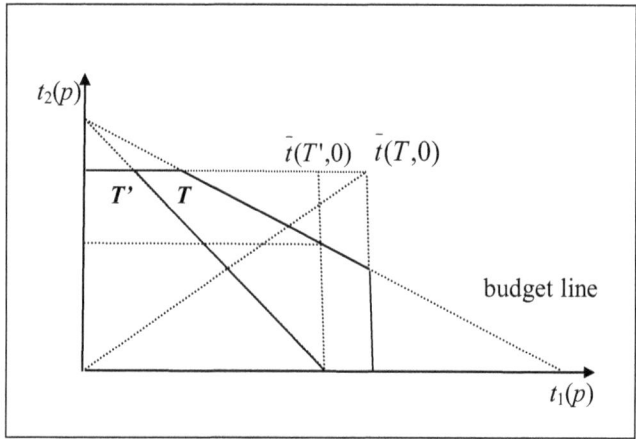

Figure 5.6: Increased claim for group 1

Doubling claims under the given budget could theoretically give full treatment to half the patients compared to the initial example (5 instead of 10 patients). This leads to a change in the budget line. To be more specific its slope becomes steeper and it shifts towards the origin which causes the set of alternatives to shrink. The relation of both groups' claims q_2/q_1 impacts the slope of the budget line. It represents the relation of medical costs in both groups. Since we look at the allocation of monetary units in the medical sector we may discuss the interchangeability of medications in both groups. Namely, the units of the medical budget could either be spent on two full treatments in group 1 or one full treatment in group 2.

As a result, we see that an increase in claims leads to greater scarcity, which we note from the shift of the budget line toward the origin. It is important to mention that we could study the same degrees of scarcity as analyzed in section 4.

From cooperative bargaining theory we may apply an axiom called individual monotonicity to the given allocation problem. When discussing changing medical claims we call the effect on treatment standards monotonicity in claims. We look at two situations $(T,0)$ and $(T',0)$ in two-dimensional space $\widetilde{B}^{2+}$ that differ only in the medical claim of group 1.

Axiom C.MON (Monotonicity in claims): Let $(T,0)$ and $(T',0)$ be two bargaining situations in $\widetilde{B}^{2+}$ with $n_j = n_j'$ for one j such that $T \subseteq T'$, then $f_i(T,0) \geq f_i(T',0)$ for $i \neq j$ with i,j =1,2.

Monotonicity in claims means that increases in patients medical claims lead to higher degrees of scarcity and changed treatment standards which will be based on the new claims. As a consequence under the given medical budget each patient receives a reduced treatment based on these new claims.

The Kalai/Smorodinsky solution is the only solution to satisfy weak Pareto optimality, scale invariance, symmetry, and restricted monotonicity in B^{2+} (compare theorem 2.2).

The Kalai/Smorodinsky solution for two patients groups should be well defined as well since all axioms are well defined on general class B^{2+} then. Since we study here subsets of situation in B^{2+} all axioms should apply on its subclass $\widetilde{B}^{2+}$ as well.

Theorem 5.3: The Kalai/Smorodinsky solution is a solution that satisfies B.WPO, B.SYM, B.INV, and C.MON on $\widetilde{B}^{2+}$.

Proof: The Kalai/Smorodinsky solution in theorem 5.3 is a well defined concept. To see that μ fulfils B.WPO, B.SYM, B.INV, and C.MON compare other proofs above.

Thus the Kalai/Smorodinsky solution fulfils all four axioms on $\widetilde{B}^{2+}$.

Next, we analyze if the property of monotonicity in claims is a property of an allocation rule.

From cooperative bargaining we know that Nash solution does not fulfill the axiom of individual monotonicity, as the it fulfils IIA which is incompatible with a monotonicity axiom. For medical allocation situation we find that the discussed property of monotonicity in claims is not fulfilled by the Nash solution. As a result, we find that changes in medical claims do not influence the allocation, the budget is shared by half except one group claims less. Reductions in treatment standards differ among groups.

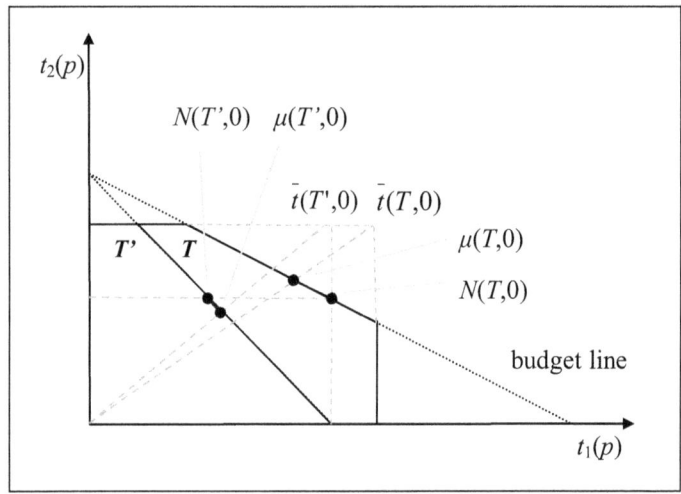

Figure 5.7: Kalai/Smorodinsky and Nash solution under monotonicity in claims

The original axiom of individual monotonicity is fulfilled by the Kalai/Smorodinsky solution. As we study subsets of allocation problems in general cooperative bargaining theory we claim that the set of axioms of the Kalai/Smorodinsky solution applies here as well. For the Kalai/Smorodinsky solution concept, we come to the conclusion that under a given budget increased medical claims per patient lead to equal proportional reduced treatment standards for each patient. In figure 5.7 the increased claim for group 1 leads to a higher degree of scarcity which affects both groups such that treatment standards respond in the same way.

Next, we study both concepts under different degrees of scarcity caused by a change in patients' claims in group 1. Figure 5.8 shows the solution paths for both concepts. Both concepts lead to different allocation outcomes, except for one case. The solutions for the degree of scarcity that we study here, which is both groups could be individually entirely treated, yields different solutions.[30] Differences result from two different allocation mechanisms. While the Nash solution shares the medical budget by half, if not one group asks less, the Kalai/Smorodinsky solution allocates the medical budget proportionally according to group size and individual claims.

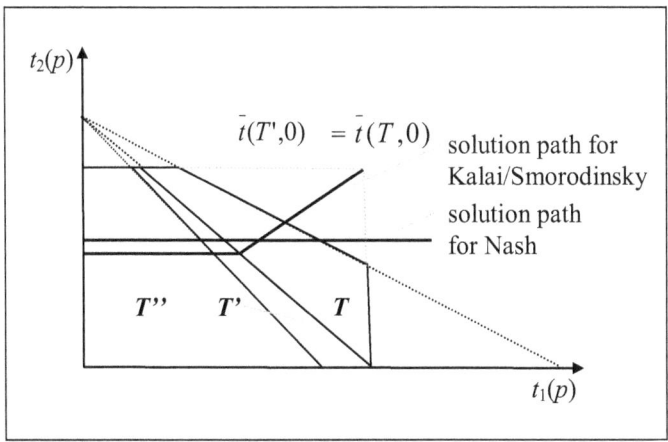

Figure 5.8: Solution Paths for Nash and Kalai/Smorodinsky solution

In detail, both solution paths run parallel until they intercept and then they are monotone increasing functions. To see this we have to find out the geometric form of the allocation problem and the geometric application of the solution mechanisms. First of all, we notice that the slope of the budget line increases with increasing claims of patients in group 1. The geometric form that arise from different claims in one group is a bundle of rays. The allocation problem has either the geometric shape of a trapezoid or a truncated trapezoid. In addition, the applied solution concepts each cut rays of the bundle in different but fix

---

[30] In Figure 10 all solution outcomes and underlying allocation situations on the upward moving line of the Kalai/Smorodinsky solution path are considered under this degree of scarcity.

proportions. For example the Nash solution is in our case the midpoint of the budget line. The Kalai/Smorodinsky solution is geometrically found as the intercept of budget line and the line connecting status quo and ideal point. Applying the first theorem on intersecting lines, we find that solution paths of both concepts must run parallel or in the special case are identical. The paths are parallel until the given budget suffice to treat more than the given number of patients in group 1. Then the application of the Kalai/Smorodinsky solution is different, since the ideal point is identical for each allocation problem. Changes in the medical claims of patients in group 2 yield equal results.

In the German statutory health system, we find often hear discussions about the implementation of new medical treatments. Most of the times the decision is based on the benefit of this therapy for patients. As long as there is a noticeable benefit new technology may be prescribed. Besides the benefit for the patients another criteria ought to be considered. Under a tight medical budget the benefit to patients under the new treatment ought to be analyzed under the aspect of financial ability and changes in treatment standards for other medical goods. The implementation of one medical treatment may exclude another. Both may be beneficial treatments yet under the given medical budget only one may be financed for all respective patients. While the Nash solution yields a sprinkler solution, the Kalai/Smorodinsky solution allocates based on claim and number of patients.

In a final step we analyze situations with decreasing claims. Theoretically we observe reversed results as with increasing claims. For example, decreasing patients' claims may be caused by decreased recommended medical quantities or sunk prices as in the case of generics. When medical prices fall due to me-to-medication or generics, then as a consequence medical resources are saved and free to be spent on other treatments. We may observe the same when patients have to pay for their medication such as nasal sprays out of their own pockets. In this case in fact patients carry part of the burden, yet public medical resources are saved for other treatments.

Concluding this section we have learned for once that increasing claims lead to higher degrees of scarcity. Here, monotonicity in claims demands that patients of all groups ought to be affected by reductions in treatment standards. Second, under the Nash solution reductions do not account for claim size and number of patients, whereas the Kalai/Smorodinsky solution does. Third, a statutory health system ought to consider monotonicity in claims since necessary reductions in claims are based on general criteria. Fourth, results for increasing claims apply to decreasing claims in the opposite way.

5.6 Results

This chapter continues the discussion of a model in chapter 4 It discusses different monotonicity properties in a medical allocation situation. Monotonicity in general explains how small changes in the initial conditions impact the outcome of an allocation problem. After motivating each change in the medical framework we applied monotonicity properties from cooperative bargaining.

We have studied how an additional patient as well as an additional patients group influence the allocation of a medical budget. These axioms are called monotonicity in number of patients and monotonicity in number of patients groups. In addition to these two types of monotonicity we analyzed how increases and decreases in the budget or in the claim of a patient change the allocation of resources. We call the axioms budget monotonicity and monotonicity in claims. As a result, we find that each change in the conditions of the model that leads to a more scarce situation means reductions in treatment standards for all patients. In detail, an additional patient or patients groups has the same impact as increased patients' claims or fewer medical resources.

In addition to the properties we studied two cooperative bargaining solution concepts in order to find out if any monotonicity property is fulfilled by either the Nash or the Kalai/Smorodinsky solution.

The famous Nash solution could not yield satisfying results on a medical allocation situation considered in this paper as none monotonicity axiom is fulfilled. It pictures a sprinkler principle this gives equal portions of the budget to each group without regarding number of patients in each group or a patient's claim size.

The Kalai/Smorodinsky on the other hand, yields a the solution that is compatible with the introduced monotonicity axioms. The proposed solution outcome reduces standard treatment proportionally such that each patient burdens equal relative reductions in standards treatment which can be legitimately claimed by each patient.

An important aspect of this work is to relate our findings to medical allocation situations under the German statutory health system.

In a statutory health system equal treatment and solidarity are important principles. For the given allocation situation the Kalai/Smorodinsky solution yields equal proportional treatment to all members patients which means equal relative burden for all patients. Especially in scarce medical allocation situation both principles become relevant.

Medical treatment to patients ought to depend on the available medical budget, on legitimate claims of patients and on the number of patients all together in order to have a self-supporting health system. If for some reason member fees yield much less medical resources than last period, then patients can expect to receive comparable but not the same treatment as last period.

In the end allocation decision to one group under a tight budget often means allocating resources to one group means cutting of treatments in another. To keep the financial system in balance and to assure equality and solidarity among members, treatment standards (patients' claims) have to be reduced proportionally as proposed by the Kalai/Smorodinsky solution.

Since we studied allocation of medical resources to groups, in a further step we could look at allocation principles within each group. We may discuss different priority criteria and their application to different medical settings. In addition to this theoretical work, we could also test in experiments and surveys if monotonicity axioms as relevant to participants as established by this model.

6 Results and outlook

In the final section we summarize the results of this work. First, we present the theoretical results of both versions of the model. We explain the property mix fulfilled by two solution concepts in both models and compare the Nash and the Kalai/Smorodinsky solutions. Second, we reflect upon properties and solutions within a medical health system. We discuss two interpretations of the solution concepts and give examples from medicine that support theoretical results. Finally, we conclude with an outlook. We discuss an application in other areas beside medicine and state further research questions.

6.1 Theoretical results of the medical allocation problem

In the basic version (chapter 3) of the model we apply bargaining theory to the simple case of two groups with one patient in each group. By assumption these two patients are representatives for patients in their groups. Here, the bargaining concepts of Nash and Kalai/Smorodinsky lead to the same unique solution. Each patient receives treatment with the probability of ½ such that a patient realizes equal (proportional) expected gains in living quality compared to the status quo. This is equivalent to equal (proportional) expected decreases in living quality compared to the ideal point. In this special case the solution concepts of Nash and Kalai/Smorodinsky represent a special egalitarian principle.

On the bargaining set of the considered two-person cases in the basic version of the model the solution mechanism of Nash and Kalai/Smorodinsky can be uniquely characterized by the properties of weak Pareto efficiency, symmetry, and invariance under positive affine transformations. In the special case of bargaining situations considered here the concepts of weak and strong Pareto optimality lead to the same allocations. According to strong Pareto efficiency, expected health states of the solution allocation can not be improved individually without decreasing another patient's health state. The property of symmetry requires that identical conditions in the allocation problem lead to identical allocations of expected living quality under the solution concept. Transformation invariance refers to applicable positive affine transformations of success probabilities of each patient individually. The stochastic solution is independent of such positive affine transformations of individual success probabilities.

In an adapted version (chapter 4 and 5), in contrast to the basic model, we introduce two groups of patients with different group size that compete for a medical budget. Applying cooperate bargaining theory to the adapted medical allocation problem, shows that now both solution concepts yield different solutions. The Nash solution concept assigns equal budgets to both groups regardless of group size as long as sharing the budget equally is efficient under the given allocation problem. On the other hand, the solution concept of Kalai/Smorodinsky assigns equal relative budgets depending on the maximum number of patients that can be treated in each group and their claims (which we call standard treatment). Interpreting the solutions of this model we find that under the second solution concept group size impacts the allocated share of the medical budget. For the Kalai/Smorodinsky solution the average allocation per person is the same in each group.

On the set of two-person cases in the adapted version of the model the above Nash solution can be characterized by the properties of weak Pareto efficiency, symmetry, invariance under positive affine transformations, and independence of irrelevant alternatives. According to weak Pareto efficiency, the number of treatments cannot be increased for both groups simultaneously. The property of symmetry requires that identical characteristics in bargaining problems of groups in the allocation problem such as requested quantities and number of patients lead to identical allocations of the medical budget. Transformation invariance refers to applicable positive affine transformations of the number of treatments. The solution of expected numbers of treatments is independent of such positive affine transformations. The fourth axiom of independence of irrelevant alternatives refers to a situation when justified claims of patients are no longer considered. According to the axiom, a solution does not change as long as the outcome to share equally is efficient.

Another set of axioms we discuss in this model are different types of monotonicity. Under the property of patient monotonicity, when a new patient requires treatment, all old patients in all groups carry the burden of the additional patient equally. Then the property of budget monotonicity requires that fewer medical resources require equal proportional reductions to each patient. Last, with the definition of standard treatment monotony, we refer to the case that the standard treatment of a patients group changes. If standard treatment demands a greater budget to one patients group, then all patients in all groups suffer an equal reduction in standard treatment.

Each type of monotonicity combined with the first three axioms of the Nash solution patient monotonicity uniquely characterizes the Kalai/Smorodinsky solution for two patients groups which results in equal proportional reductions to all patients groups.

In addition to two-person models we studied the n-group version of the Kalai/Smorodinsky solution. While the extension of the Nash solution for more than two groups is not problematic, the extension of the Kalai/Smorodinsky solution is not straight forward. Roth (1979) shows the incompatibility of the solution as defined by Kalai and Smorodinsky (1977). On the other hand, there are different sets of properties that characterize this concept e.g. by Thomson and Lensberg (1989). The authors use a property called population monotonicity that we translate to patients group monotonicity. Together with weak Pareto optimality, invariance of positive affine transformation, anonymity and continuity it characterizes the Kalai/Smorodinsky solution for more than two patients groups. Monotonicity in patients groups implies that when another group of patients requests medical treatment this group's claim is equally regarded which means that the claims of all other groups have to be reduced proportionally. Weak Pareto optimality and invariance of positive affine transformation are identical to their explanations in the 2-group case. Anonymity expresses that names of the patients or group are not relevant to the solution outcome. Finally, continuity requires that small changes in the initial conditions lead to small changes in the solution.

All presented solutions from cooperative bargaining theory constitute different egalitarian concepts. The Nash and the Kalai/Smorodinsky solutions in the basic version of the model as well as the Nash solution in the adapted version reflect an equal split distribution for both groups. The Kalai/Smorodinsky solution in the second version on the other hand, reflects an equal share distribution proportional to group size. In comparison of the two versions of the presented model, we find that including group size as a distribution criteria impacts the solution. Recognizing the actual number of patients results in equal medical allocations per patient.

6.2 Interpreting the results within a medical context

Under the given allocation problem we discuss medical implications of the presented theoretical results for the basic version. The solution to receive treatment with probability of one half refers to a health level that is reached under both solution concepts. The allocation problem is such that not all patients can be treated in order to have the desired health level due to lack of medical resources. The interpretation of that results admits two possibilities. First, the chance to be treated is ½ . Therefore, the chance to reach the desired health level is also ½. In consequence this interpretation means that half the patients remain without treatment. Second, another possibility is that all patients may reach a higher health level compared to status quo yet not the desired level as discussed before. If the budget is split equally to both groups then each group may assign an equal amount to each patient. In total, we realize a situation in which both groups realize a higher health level as in the status quo, yet the attained levels are different in both groups.

The applied solution concepts in the adapted version propose different feasible allocations of the budget. Under the Nash solution the budget is split equally as long as this is efficient, the result is that allocations per patient are different in both patients groups. This concept fails to account for the actual number of patients in each group and rejecting this important information leads to different allocated amounts for each group. In the end an equal distribution to groups results in a discrimination of patients in that group.

The Kalai/Smorodinsky solution acknowledges this aspect in a proportional allocation solution which yields the same proportional reductions of standard treatment. All group claims are reduced in the same proportion. Group size matters, solution is fair in so far that reductions are equal in proportions to all patients. The solution concept contributes to distributional fairness.

So far we discussed two versions and their interpretations. While the interpretation of the basic version is related to expected health states, the adapted version pictures the allocation of a medical budget. Both version are interchangeable in their interpretation if we assume that the concept of standard treatment enables patients to medical services that assure equal health states. In addition, we can translate between interpretations in a linear way.

Though we may interpret the results in both versions in the same way, we have distinct their interpretation with respect to recognizing group size. In the basic version group size is not recognized. While in the adapted version of the model the number of patients is an allocation criteria it is differently considered by the applied solution concepts. The Nash solution as in the basic version allocates independent of group size, in contrast to the Kalai/Smorodinsky solution that allocates equally proportional amounts of the medical budget.

In conclusion, we state that the allocation mechanism of the Kalai/Smorodinsky solution pictures an important property to reach an agreement in medical allocation situations. For example, if the medical budget in a hospital falls short by 10% as compared to last year, then each medical department ought to receive a reduction in allocation by 10% compared to last year. Equal reduction in proportion may rather result in an agreement as cutting allocations by different percentages if the claims of all departments are regarded equally legitimate.

It is an important result that the Kalai/Smorodinsky solution concepts supports for distributional justice. In this sense, if we have to reduce standard treatment or desired health states due to restricted budget, then all ought to carry the same burden.

In addition to interpreting the results of both solution concepts we state the importance of some properties for a medical allocation problem that may or may not be regarded desirable. First, light properties that characterize the Kalai/Smorodinsky solution and the Nash solution. Invariance, enables us to go back and forth in units of treatment chances and health states or budget and treatments as long as we refer to a positive affine transformation. In the end it does not matter if we discuss allocating the medical budget or the number of full treatments. Weak Pareto optimality requires that all resources are used up and no more treatments are feasible. An important criteria, for example if no agreement can be found. Failing to reach an agreement on the allocation of the budget is therefore inefficient. Symmetry assures that medical budget is not allocated on the basis of names of the patients or social status, income etc.

Second, we light different monotonicity axioms as fulfilled by the Kalai/Smorodinsky solution. The property of patients monotonicity this means equal relative burden for all old patients to accommodate new patients. This result strengthens important principles of a statutory health system - equal treatment and solidarity. The property of budget monotonicity states that medical treatment to patients ought to depend on the available medical budget, on legitimate claims of patients and on the number of patients all together in order to have a financially self-supporting health system. Next, the property of standard treatment monotonicity illustrates the necessary trade-off in allocating scarce medical resources. An allocation decision in favor of one group under a tight budget means cutting-back on treatments in another.

Last, we come to a property that is in contrast to all other discussed properties not desirable – independence of irrelevant alternatives. The property considers irrelevant alternatives as equal to relevant alternatives, which is not adequate in this medical allocation problem. Irrelevant alternatives in this context refers to allocations to patients that might be treated. So we have allocation alternatives with patients that ask treatment in competition with allocation to fictitious patients. Considering irrelevant alternatives leads to different per patients allocation in both groups. In the discuss model we see no reason why these two types of allocation alternatives are to be regarded equally. It is because of this conflict that we do not favor the result of the Nash solution.

Pointing out the advantages of the Kalai/Smorodinsky solution and the different properties that characterize this concept, we discuss the two possible interpretations of that result in detail. First, we may give standard treatment to some patients, which means some patients do not receive medical treatment. Second, we give some treatment to all patients, yet the scope of treatment is reduced compared to standard treatment.

The first proposal of denying treatment to some patients seems unethical, even unlawful. For what reason can we legitimately exclude some patients from treatment? From our model we regard patients in one group equal with respect to their illness and their claims. Within that scope of the model there is no objective reason for discrimination. There might be a criteria such as age, social responsibility, or compliance that allow for a discrimination of patients. Yet this has do be discussed in another model.

The second proposal of reducing standard treatment reflects the idea to treat all patients equally. The notion of standard treatment encompasses all necessary medical treatments in order to reach the best health state for each patient. It enables patients to treatment according to medical guidelines which includes the latest progress in medicine that is beneficial to the patient.

The question is if such a health status can be secured to everyone due to medical shortages in the existing social health system. What if receiving the best health level to all is impossible because of restrictions in the medical budget or problems in medication such as vaccine or organ transplants. Within the model we focus on the monetary restriction, and assume that medicine is available as needed. Solving this problem we need a public discourse in order to determine a standard reference health status and services that are appropriate and necessary to attain this level. In addition we need to think of the reference health status as a level that can be attained with the given financial resources in the medical sector.

The answer to medical allocation problems as discussed in this work is to share scarce resources such that each patient carries an equal proportion of the shortage of the medical budget. If keeping the financial system in balance and assuring equality and solidarity among members of a statutory health system are regarded important qualities, treatment standards ought to be reduced proportionally as proposed by the Kalai/Smorodinsky solution.

The consequences of the reduction to each patient can be different for each medical allocation situation. In hospitals reducing standard treatment may mean to cut treatment time per patient. For doctors this means to reduce the time to visit, examine and treat patients as well as for nurses this means to reduce the amount of nursing time, even to reduce cleaning time. This example enables proportional reduction of standard treatment, as time per patient can be reduced proportionally. But how much can they be reduced? This question induces a discussion about minimal treatment standards for patients in the hospital. Additionally needed services may require co-payments and private insurance that pays for special doctor visits, single bedrooms and special nursing time. Again, the question comes up, how far can we reduce statutory services to patients that cannot afford private insurance. If reducing treatment time is considered, may be we have to discuss a substitution of services. For example, reducing treatment time per visit with a doctor, while allowing nurses to take care of some specialized treatments in the laboratory, take blood pressure and blood samples, help with bookkeeping, organize an efficient allocation of appointments etc. Other medical area one of the following methods may be applied. Postponing of medical services surgery etc, as well as longer waiting time for doctor's appointment are popular methods for pushing cost to the next period when medical supply is scarce. Medication and medical services may be excluded from the treatment catalogue in case there cannot be proven an significant additional benefit to the patient. In general co-payments are regarded popular in terms of self-determination of patients.

6.3 Outlook

Finally, sum up this work with a reflection on the scope of model discussed here. We shortly discuss its application in other areas. In addition, we mention further research questions as revealed by our work.

The application of bargaining concepts as done in this work is not restricted to medical allocation problems. We find similar allocation problems in other areas of decision making and bargaining. Originally these models pictured wage negotiation between employer and employee. The allocation rules that is proposed by the two concepts may well be applied in other area of private and public interests, for example, reducing public spending on the level of the public federal budget with the demand that each resort reduces spending by a certain percentage. This may proceed down to the bottom where decisions about projects and spending are finalized. Beside health, education, culture, environment are of important public interest. Allocation problems within these areas of public spending are no different from medical allocation problems as discussed here. There are different projects that are funded in education: kindergarten, preschool, elementary schools, high schools and university... . Each single resort may be covered by the budget, yet financing all is impossible. The approach by Kalai/Smorodinsky imposes saving money through small cuts in all projects. Instead of realizing a large new building of a gymnasium we may chose a smaller less costly version.

In the same manner we may apply this concept to such allocation problems in business and private lives.

Before concluding this work we give an overview of research question as imposed by the results of this model.

First, we concentrated on the allocation result to different patients groups. The allocation process within these groups has not been regarded so far. It may another question to study different allocation mechanisms with groups such as discussing prioritizing criteria.

A further step may be the another extension to more than two groups of patients. The generalization of the Nash solution will probably be straight forward. However, the property of strong Pareto efficiency is problematic for the concept of Kalai/Smorodinsky with more than two groups as it is with more than two persons (Roth (1979)). We will probably have to apply a lexicographic solution concept (c.f. Imai (1983)). This implies that first the claims of all patients in all groups are satisfied according to some egalitarian principle that still needs to be derived. Afterwards the expected health states of some patients can be increased further on in order to achieve Pareto optimality. This contributes to the discussion of minimal claims and basic treatment within a health system. Beside the theoretical work on applying bargaining concepts from cooperative game theory, another approach is to test these solution concepts experimentally. It may be interesting to study choices of either allocation mechanism in a medical settings and to analyze which is preferred by the involved participants.

Scientific references

Ahlert, Marlies (2005): Priorities in Allocations with Thresholds, preliminary version of a Discussion Paper, September 20th 2005, Department of Law and Economics Martin-Luther-University Halle-Wittenberg.

Ahlert, Marlies (2006): Discrete Allocation of a Divisible Good – Allocation of Chances, Discussion Papers in Economics, No.50, Department of Law and Economics Martin-Luther-University Halle-Wittenberg.

Ahlert, Marlies (2009): If not only Numbers Count – Allocation of Equal Chances. Rationality, markets and morals, in: Perspectives in moral sciences, Michael Baurmann/Bernd Lahno (eds.), Vol.0, pp.183-197.

Ahlert, Marlies/ Stefan Felder/ Bodo Vogt (2012): Which Patients Do I Treat? – An Experimental Study with Economists and Physicians, Health Economics Review, Vol.2, pp.1-25.

Ahlert, Marlies/ Katja Funke/ Lars Schwettmann (2012): Thresholds, productivity, and context: an experimental study on determinants of distributive behavior, Social Choice and Welfare, URL: http://www.priorisierung-in-der-medizin.de/documents/FOR655_Nr25_Ahlert.pdf.

Ahlert, Marlies/ Wolfgang Granigg/ Gertrud Greif-Higer/ Hartmut Kliemt/ Gerd Otto (2008): Prioritätsänderungen in der Allokation postmortaler Spenden-Lebern - Grundsätzliche und aktuelle Fragen, in: Priorisierung in der Medizin – Interdisziplinäre Forschungsansätze, Michael Freitag/Walther A. Wohlgemuth (eds.), MWV 2009.

Binmore, Ken (1991): Fun and Games: A Textbook on Game theory, D.C. Heath.

Binmore, Ken; Ariel Rubinstein, Asher Wolinsky, (1986): The Nash bargaining solution in economic modelling, in: RAND Journal of Economics, Vol.17, No.2, pp.176-188.

Bossert, Walter (1992): Monotonic solutions for bargaining with claims, in: Economic Letters, Vol.39, Issue 4, pp.395-399.

Brams, Steven J./ Alan D. Taylor (1996): Fair division: from cake-cutting to dispute resolution, Cambridge University Press.

Breyer, Friedrich/ Peter Zweifel/ Mathias Kifmann (2005): Gesundheitsökonomik, 5. überarbeitete Auflage, Springer.

Chun, Youngsub/ William Thomson (1992): Bargaining problems with claims, in: Mathematical Social Sciences, Vol.24, Issue 1, pp.19-33.

Dannecker, Gerhard/ Stefan Huster/ Christian Katzenmeier/ André Bohmeier/ Björn Schmitz-Luhn/ Anne Franziska Streng (2009): Priorisierung: notwendiger rechtlicher Gestaltungsspielraum, in: Deutsches Ärzteblatt, Jg. 106, Heft 41, S.A2007-A2010,
URL: http://www.aerzteblatt.de/v4/archiv/pdf.asp?id=66226 .

Diederich, Adele/ Petra Lietz/ Marina Otten/ Maike Schnoor/ Margrit Schreier/ Jessica Schröter/ Jeannette Winkelhage/ Norman Wirsik (2009): Fragebogen zur Erhebung von Präferenzen in der Bevölkerung bezüglich der Verteilung von Gesundheitsleistung in der GKV, in Schriftenreihe FOR655, Nr. 18,
URL:http://www.priorisierung-in-der-medizin.de/documents/ FOR655_Nr18_ Diederich.pdf .

Drabinski, Thomas (2008): Gesundheitsfonds ante portas, in: Schriftenreihe Institut für Mikrodatenanalyse, Band 12.

Eichberger, Jürgen (1993): Game theory for economists, Academic Press.

Eisenmenger, Matthias/ Olga Pötzsch/ Bettina Sommer (2006): Bevölkerung Deutschlands bis 2050 - 11. koordinierte Bevölkerungsvorausberechnung, Hrg.: Statistisches Bundesamt, Wiesbaden.

Fisher, Roger/ Ury, William L. (1999): Getting to yes: negotiating an agreement without giving in, Random House.

Fuchs, Christoph/ Eckhard Nagel/ Heiner Raspe (2009): Rationalisierung, Rationierung und Priorisierung – was ist gemeint?, in: Deutsches Ärzteblatt, Jg.106, Heft 12, S.A 554-557,
URL: http://www.aerzteblatt.de/v4/archiv/artikel.asp?id=63854 .

Friedrich, Daniel R./ Alena M. Buyx/ Bettina Schöne-Seifert (2009): Priorisierung: Marginale Wirksamkeit als Ausschlusskriterium, in: Deutsches Ärzteblatt, Vol.106, Heft 31-32, S. A1562-1564,
URL: http://www.aerzteblatt.de/v4/archiv/artikel.asp?id=65534 .

Gauthier, David (1986): Morals by agreement, Oxford University Press.

Graf von der Schulenburg, J.-Matthias/ Oliver Schöffski (1993): Kosten-Nutzen-Analysen im Gesundheitswesen, in: Soziale Gerechtigkeit im Gesundheitswesen: ökonomische, ethische, rechtliche Fragen am Beispiel der Transplantationsmedizin, Eckhardt Nagel/ Christoph Fuchs (eds.), pp.168-182.

Güth, Werner/ Rolf Schmittberger/ Bernd Schwarze (1982): An experimental analysis of ultimatum bargaining, in: Journal of Economic Behavior and Organization, Vol.3, pp.367-388.

Harsanyi, John C. (1956): Approaches to the bargaining problem before and after the theory of games: a critical discussion of Zeuthen's Hick's, and Nash's theories, in Econometrica, Vol.24, No.2, pp.144-157.

Huster, Stefan (2005): Sozialstaat oder soziale Gerechtigkeit? Zum Spannungsverhältnis von politischer Philosophie und Verfassungsrecht am Beispiel der Altersrationierung im Gesundheitssystem, in: Juristische Grundlagenforschung, (ARSP-Beiheft Nr. 104), Robert Alexy (Hrsg.), 2005, S. 202 - 217.

Imai, Haruo (1983): Individual Monotonicity and Lexicographic Maximin Solution, in: Econometrica, Vol. 51, No. 2, pp. 389-401.

Kagel, John H./ Alvin E. Roth (1995): Handbook of Experimental Economics, Princeton University Press, Princeton.

Kahneman, Daniel/ Amos Tversky (1979): Prospect Theory: An Analysis of Decision under Risk, in: Econometrica, Vol.47, No.2, pp.263 – 292.

Kalai, Ehud (1977): Nonsymmetric Nash solution and replications of 2-person bargaining, in: International Journal of Game Theory, Vol.3, Issue 3, pp.129-133.

Kalai, Ehud/ Meir Smorodinsky (1975): Other Solutions to Nash's Bargaining Problems, Econometrica, Vol.43, pp.513 – 518.

Kifmann, Mathias/ Marlies Ahlert (2009): Bewertung von Kosten- und Nutzen in der gesetzlichen Krankenversicherung. Einstellung der Versicherten. In: Gesundheitsmonitor 2009 - Gesundheitsversorgung und Gestaltungsoptionen aus der Perspektive der Bevölkerung, J. Bröcken et al. (eds.), Gütersloh 2009, pp.239-257.

Keun, Friedrich/ Roswitha Prott (2008): Einführung in die Krankenhauskostenrechnung, Gabler.

Klemisch-Ahlert, Marlies (1996): Bargaining in Economic and Ethical Environments - An Experimental Study and Normative Solution Concepts, Springer.

Lübbe, Weyma (2004): Tödliche Entscheidung: Allokation von Leben und Tod in Zwangslagen, Mentis.

Luce, Duncan R./ Howard Raiffa (1975), Games and Decisions: Introduction and Critical Survey, Dover Publications.

Lüdeke, Reinar/ Hanjo Allinger (2005): Grenzüberschreitende Leistungen im Gesundheitswesen - Eine volkswirtschaftliche Analyse von Leistungs- und Finanzierungsstrukturen im Grenzgebiet zwischen Bayern und Oberösterreich. Band 3: Der Krankenhausbereich, Eine Untersuchung im Auftrag der AOK-Bayern und der Oberösterreichischen Gebietskrankenkasse, Institut für empirische Wirtschafts- und Sozialforschung.

Moulin, Hervé (2004): Fair distribution and collective welfare, MIT.

Nagel, Eckhardt/ Christoph Fuchs (Hrsg.) (1993): Soziale Gerechtigkeit im Gesundheitswesen: ökonomische, ethische, rechtliche Fragen am Beispiel der Transplantationsmedizin, Springer.

Nash, John F. Jr. (1950): The Bargaining Problem, in: Econometrica, Vol.18, No.2, pp.155-162.

Nydegger, Rudy V./ Guillermo Owen (1975): Two Person Bargaining: An Experimental Test of the Nash Axioms, in: International Journal of Game Theory, Vol.3, pp.239-349.

Ostrom, Elinor (1990): Governing the commons: the evolution of institutions for collective actions, Cambridge.

Parfit, Derek (1978): Innumerate Ethics, in: Philosophy and Public Affairs, Vol. 7(4), pp.285 - 301.

Raiffa, Howard/ John Richardson/ David Metcalf (2007): Negotiation analysis: the science and art of collaborative decision making, Prentice Hall India.

Ramme, Manfred/ Ullrich Vetter (2002): Die Bildung von Abteilungsbudgets auf der Basis von AP-DRG's, in: f&w, Vol.17, Heft 02/2002, pp.156-158.

Roemer, John E. (1998): Theories of distributive justice, Harvard University Press.

Roth, Alvin E. (1979): Axiomatic Models of Bargaining, eds: Beckmann, M; Künzi, H.P., Springer.

Rubinstein, Ariel (1982): Perfect equilibrium in a bargaining model, in: Econometrica Vol.50, No.1, pp.97-109.

Stevens, Carl. M. (1958): On the theory of negotiation, in: The Quarterly Journal of Economics, Vol.72, pp.77-97.

Taurek, John (1977): Should the numbers count?, in: Philosophy and Public Affairs, Vol.6, pp.293 – 316.

Thompson, Leigh (2005): The mind and heart of the negotiator, Prentice Hall.

Thomson, William (1994): Cooperative Models of Bargaining, in: Handbook of Game Theory with Economic Applications, Robert J. Aumann/ Sergiu Hart (eds), Elsevier Science, pp.1237 - 1284.

Thomson, William/ Terje Lensberg (1989): Axiomatic Theory of Bargaining with a variable number of agents, Cambridge University Press.

Yaari, Menahem E./ Maya Bar Hillel (1984): On dividing justly, in: Social Choice and Welfare, Vol.1, pp.1-24.

Young, Peiton (1994): Equity in theory and practice, Princeton University Press.

Younis, Mustafa Z./ Dana A. Forgione (2009): The relationship between the Balanced Budget Act and length of stay for Medicare patients in US hospitals, European Journal of Health Economics, pp. 1057–1063.

Zeuthen, Frederick (1930): Problems of monopoly and economic welfare, Routledge.

Zimmermann, Jana (2009): Modellierung von Priorisierungsregeln am Spezialfall der Triage, in: Priorisierung in der Medizin – Interdisziplinäre Forschungsansätze, Michael Freitag/Walther A. Wohlgemuth (eds), MWV.

General references

AOK-Bundesverband, Rabattverträge 2009-2011, Berlin, 2009,
URL: http://www.aok-gesundheitspartner.de/inc_ges/download/dl.php/bundes verband/apotheke/imperia/md/content/gesundheitspartner/bund/arztundpraxis/ar zneimittel/aok_rabatt_faqs_240709.pdf .

BKK Landesverband Hessen, Geschäftsbericht 2008 des BKK Landesverbandes Hessen, Frankfurt am Main, 2009,
URL: http://www.bkk-hessen.de/oppromedia/zahlen/gb2008.pdf .

Bundesinstitut für Arzneimittel und Medizinprodukte, Bearbeitungsstatistik: Zulassungs- und Registrierungsanträge, Bonn, April 2010,
URL: http://www.bfarm.de/cln_012/nn_424552/SharedDocs/Publikationen/DE/ Arzneimittel/4__statistik/stat-2010-internet-apr,templateId=raw,property=publi cationFile.pdf/stat-2010-internet-apr.pdf .

Bundesministerium für Gesundheit, Daten des Gesundheitswesens 2009, Berlin, 2009.
URL:http://www.bmg.bund.de/SharedDocs/Publikationen/DE/Daten-des-Gesundheitswesens2009,templateId=raw,property=publicationFile.pdf/Daten-des-Gesundheitswesens2009.pdf .

Bundesministerium für Gesundheit, Gesetzliche Krankenversicherung vorläufige Rechnungsergebnisse 4. Quartal 2009, Berlin, April 2010,
URL:http://www.bmg.bund.de/cln_169/nn_1168278/SharedDocs/Downloads/D E/Statistiken/Gesetzliche-Krankenversicherung/Finanzergebnisse/KV-45-4-Quartal-2009,templateId=raw,property=publicationFile.pdf/KV-45-4-Quartal-2009.pdf .

Bundesministerium für Gesundheit: Gesundheitsreform 2007 im Überblick, Berlin, 2009,
URL: http://www.bmg.bund.de/cln_178/nn_1168258/SharedDocs/Standardarti kel/ DE/AZ/G/Glossarbegriff-Gesundheitsreform.html?__nnn=true .

Bundesministerium für Gesundheit, GKV-Beitragssatzverordnung vom 29.10.2008, Berlin, 2008
URL: http://www.bmg.bund.de/cln_151/nn_1168248/SharedDocs/Downloads/ DE/Standardartikel/G/Glossar-Gesundheitsfonds/Verordnung-Beitragssaetze-29-10-08 .

Bundesregierung Deutschland, Gutachten 2009 des Sachverständigenrates zur Begutachtung der Entwicklung im Gesundheitswesen: Koordination und Integration – Gesundheitsversorgung in einer Gesellschaft des längeren Lebens, Drucksache:16/13770, Berlin, 2009,
URL: http://dip21.bundestag.de/dip21/btd/16/137/1613770.pdf .

Bundesversicherungsamt, Festlegungen für das Ausgleichsjahr 2011, Bonn, downloaded June 7th 2010,
URL (4 documents): http://www.bundesversicherungsamt.de/cln_153/nn_1046746/DE/Risikostrukturausgleich/Festlegungen/festlegungen__node.html?__nnn=true .

Bundeszentrale für politische Bildung, Gesundheitspolitik, Bonn, downloaded February 10th 2010:
URL: http://www.bpb.de/themen/X9C5R7,0,0,Gesundheitspolitik.

Deutscher Ethikrat, Pressemitteilung 05/2008: Deutscher Ethikrat startet Beratungen zum Problemfeld der Ressourcenallokation im Gesundheitswesen, Berlin, September 25th 2008,
URL: http://www.ethikrat.org/dateien/pdf/PM_2008_05.pdf .

FOR 655 "Priorisierung in der Medizin", downloaded June 8th 2010, Bremen,
URL: www.priorisierung-in-der-medizin.de .

Gesundheitsberichterstattung des Bundes, Einsparpotential der 30 umsatzstärksten Analogpräparate in 2008,
Datenquelle: GKV-Arzneimittelindex, Wissenschaftliches Institut der AOK, Bonn, downloaded June 6th 2010,

URL: http://www.gbe-bund.de/oowa921-install/servlet/oowa/aw92/ dboowasys 921.xwdevkit/xwd_init?gbe.isgbetol/xs_start_neu/&p_aid=i&p_aid=60236873 &nummer=604&p_sprache=D&p_indsp=-&p_aid=79727971 .

GKV-Spitzenverband: Anzahl der Krankenkassen im Zeitablauf – Konzentrationsprozess durch Fusionen, Berlin, April 2010, URL:http://www.gkv-spitzenverband.de/upload/Krankenkassen_Fusionen verlauf_2010-03_01_2000_12796.jpg .

GKV-Spitzenverband: So entstehen Arzneimittelpreise in der europäischen Union, Berlin, downloaded June 6th 2010, URL: http://www.gkv-spitzenverband.de/upload/Arzneimittelpreise .

IMS Health 2010: IMS Marktbericht: Entwicklung des Pharmamarktes im Dezember und Jahr 2009, Frankfurt am Main, 2010, URL:http://www.imshealth.de/sixcms/media.php/16/Kommentierte%20Grafike n %20IMS%20Marktbericht%2012_2009.14568.pdf .

Institut für das Entgeltsystem im Krankenhaus, Fallpauschalenkatalog 2010, Siegburg, 2010,
URL: http://www.g-drg.de/cms/index.php/inek_site_de/G-DRG-System_2010 /Fallpauschalen-Katalog/Fallpauschalen-Katalog_2010 .

Institut für Qualität und Wirtschaftlichkeit im Gesundheitswesen, URL: http://www.iqwig.de/.

Kassenärztliche Bundesvereinigung, Rabatte und Rabattverträge, Berlin, downloaded June 8th 2010,
URL: http://www.kbv.de/ais/12909.html .

Marburger Bund, Tarifkonflikt Ärzte/VKA, downloaded June 6th 2010, URL: www.marburger-bund.de .

Zentrale Ethikkommission bei der Bundesärztekammer, Prioritäten in der medizinischen Versorgung im System der Gesetzlichen Krankenversicherung: Müssen und können wir uns entscheiden? Berlin, 2000,
URL: http://www.zentrale-ethikkommission.de/page.asp?his=0.1.24 .

Zentrale Ethikkommission bei der Bundesärztekammer, Priorisierung medizinischer Leistungen im System der Gesetzlichen Krankenversicherung, Berlin, 2007,
URL: http://www.zentrale-ethikkommission.de/page.asp?his=0.1.53 .

www.ingramcontent.com/pod-product-compliance
Ingram Content Group UK Ltd.
Pitfield, Milton Keynes, MK11 3LW, UK
UKHW021836210426
5322IPUK00021B/318